WALKING THE DIVIDE

A Tale of a Journey Home

SANG-E-MEEL PUBLICATIONS
LAHORE — PAKISTAN

923.50   H. Khan
            Walking the Divide: A Tale of a Journey
Home / Halima Khan. - Lahore: Sang-e-Meel
Publications, 2021.
            192 pp.
            1. Biography & Memoirs.
I. Title.

© **Halima Khan**

Edited by Mariam Sarwar and Safia Aftab
Cover Art by Yashar Sumair Tarar

2021
Published by:
Afzaal Ahmad
Sang-e-Meel Publications,
Lahore.

Disclaimer

The findings, interpretations and conclusions expressed in this book are entirely those of the author and / or the narrator and should not be attributed to Sang-e-Meel Publications.

ISBN-10:   969-35-33361-5
ISBN-13:   978-969-35-3361-3

Sang-e-Meel Publications

25 Shahrah-e-Pakistan (Lower Mall), Lahore-54000 PAKISTAN
http://www.sangemeel.com e-mail: smp@sangemeel.com

DEDICATED to the memory of Syed Sardar Ahmad,

To all those who WALKED THE DIVIDE,

Cheated death,

Barely escaped survival,

To cross over.

Preface

The impact of the Pakistan Movement culminated not only in the emergence of the world's largest Muslim country but also proved to be a stepping stone for the independence of many other colonized nations in different parts of the world on the basis of the right of self-determination. The creation of Pakistan was not an ordinary event but a miracle that happened in extremely unfavourable circumstances. In my view, the establishment of our country was the will of Allah the Almighty, who chose Quaid-e-Azam Muhammad Ali Jinnah to accomplish this gigantic task. He was not a mere politician, but an unmatchable statesman. Allah Almighty had bestowed upon him rare qualities of farsightedness and the capability of making right decisions at the right time. His life history from childhood up to the establishment of a separate homeland for the Muslims of the sub-continent testifies that nature had groomed him very well to become the saviour of the followers of His beloved Prophet Muhammad (PBUH) living in this region, which was polluted with idolatry and polytheism.

During the struggle for Pakistan, Muslims could have never imagined that to achieve their sacred goal, they would have to cross the streams of blood and tears. Due to the partial and inept British administration, the Muslim population of the sub-continent had to bear unparalleled agony and bloodbath at the hands of violent Hindu and Sikh mobs. The eyewitness accounts of their suffering are not only soul-shaking but also a bitter reminder that the foundations of Pakistan are saturated with the blood of around one million Muslim men, women, and innocent children who were brutally murdered on their way to a separate homeland.

The book in hand, "WALKING THE DIVIDE: A Tale of Journey Home," amply defines the magnitude of the events of Partition. It is a story of a twenty-one-year-old young man Syed Sardar Ahmad who was forced to leave his ancestral home in

Kharkhoda, a town in District Rohtak along with his family members. While migrating to Pakistan, he had to travel for nineteen consecutive days, during which his family suffered a lot. He was the only surviving member of his large family who succeeded in entering Pakistan. The unbearable mental and physical torture of this journey could never be washed away from his memory.

His memories, presented in this work, though very painful, can become a source of inspiration and devotion for our new generation, whose knowledge about the historical freedom movement and the circumstances under which Pakistan came into being is getting limited day by day.

In the context of the current Hindutva movement in India, this book is a testimony that Quaid-e-Azam's Two-Nation Theory was correct. I congratulate its team on bringing out this valuable book of historical significance and hope they will further explore those hidden aspects of our national history which are still not touched by researchers and historians.

No doubt, the contents of this book will motivate readers, particularly the sensitive ones, to have a critical self-analysis towards seeing whether their attitude towards Pakistan is compatible with the sufferings and sacrifices made by their forefathers during Partition. I pray to Allah Almighty that He may grant Barrister Syed Sardar Ahmad the highest place in Jannat ul Firdous (Ameen).

Chief Justice(r) Mian Mahboob Ahmed
Chairman Pakistan Movement Workers Trust

Part I

Part 1

Syed Sardar Ahmad:

"As-salāmu ʿalaykum, my name is Syed Sardar Ahmad. I was born on the 6th of October 1926 in Delhi, at Qamar Manzil in Sita Ram Bazaar. Qamar Manzil was my mother's family home. Her father, my nana, was Justice Khwaja Mehmood Hosain, a civil judge. My mother's name was Riffat Bano. She was a homemaker. My father's name was Syed Sharif Ahmad. His ancestors were from Kharkhoda in East Punjab's district Rohtak, which is around 20 miles from Delhi. My father owned land in Rohtak, and his occupation was farming.

Kharkhoda is in a rainy area, so most of the houses there were made of concrete. Our house was made of concrete, too, a big bungalow across five acres of land.

There were some cars on the roads of India in 1926, but not in *Sita Ram Bazaar*. The streets of that *bazaar* — lined by houses and shops, were barely wide enough for four or five persons to walk side by side."

Through these streets on the 6th of October, the call to morning prayer floated gently from a slim minaret. Men in prayer caps walked in and out of the mosque — at a little shop beside it, a sleepy old man lifted puffy golden *puris* from a large wok and placed them in plates of *cholay*. Several men stopped by for breakfast. They ate on benches, idly observing the people on the street: men wearing *kurta pyjama* — others in turbans and crisp white *dhotis*. The few women who passed by were clad in colourful *saris* or *ghagras*. A cleaner squatted between his broom and bucket opposite the shop, smoking his first *beedi* of the day.

The other stores were closed, their low wooden doors fastened with large padlocks. One shop, which was little more than a wooden platform, was equipped with a weighing scale where people brought in bulks of old newspapers to exchange for cash or small items such as rice cakes.

There was a store selling fabric, fancy *parandas* for braiding hair and *gota* to adorn clothes. When open, it was long and so narrow that there was barely room for one customer to pass behind another. The light from several lanterns barely reached the furthest end.

Tucked away in a side lane was a blacksmith who fixed harnesses and mended pots and pans amidst loud clangs, smoke and fire, and a farrier who shod horses. The animals were led up to the shop and tied to a post outside where they stood with their noses in bags of feed while the blacksmith inspected their hooves, removed worn-out shoes and nailed on new ones.

An apothecary further up from the mosque dispensed medicines and dental services, as advertised by a poster on which a man showed off an unconvincing set of teeth while grimacing in pain or delight, it was impossible to tell.

Doors of all the houses in this *bazaar* opened straight onto the street, with one exception: a sturdy brown gate with a narrow side door set in a high brick wall. It belonged to a *haveli* which was at quite a distance from the lane. The gate and the side door in the wall were studded with metal knobs. Engraved onto a pillar beside the gate was the name of the *haveli*, *Qamar Manzil*. Underneath, a plaque proclaimed that the house belonged to Justice Khwaja Mehmood Hosain.

The graceful arches resting on slender pillars on the upper floor of the *haveli* were visible from a distance. The windows fronted by *jharokhas*, delicately carved screens, were for the ladies of the house to view the street discreetly, without being seen themselves.

The residents of the house usually went back to sleep after morning prayers, but early that morning, the light was still not extinguished in several of the rooms. As the sun rose a little higher, the small side door in the boundary wall opened, and a man hurried out, shouldering a cloth bag. He was followed by another man carrying a *chaaba* — a shallow, wide basket — upon his head. The basket was covered with coloured paper tied around with gold and silver ribbons. The first man allowed the second to get ahead of him, reached back, shut the door, and then caught up with his companion. Overtaking him, he walked in haste, dodging pedestrians and the odd cow and goat wandering free. In just a few minutes, both men had passed the *bazaar* to a wider road.

The two men walked into an open space that was hemmed in on three sides by buildings. Several small stalls and a couple of *tongas* dotted the far end, and some men squatted beside the smouldering remains of a fire, mugs of tea in their hands. Others were asleep on mats under a tree, their faces covered with turbans or *chaddars* to keep the flies off. A strong smell of horse dung filled the air.

The men from the *haveli* skirted the *tongas* and walked towards a couple of cars parked at a safe distance from hooves. One of them opened the back door of a black Canadian Ford, and the other placed the basket on the seat.

"The best sweetmeats in all of India," he muttered, adjusting the basket securely so the covered-in-*warq laddu*, *barfi*, and *rasgullay* would not roll out. He slammed the door shut and rubbed his arms, "*Uff.*"

"*Ghar jao ab,*" the other man asked him to go back home now.

11

"Maybe you can still get some rest."

His companion rolled his eyes, "With a new baby in the house? You must be joking. There'll be people coming to congratulate Judge *Sahib* and see his grandson all week." He raised his hand to bid farewell, "*Allah hafiz*, my friend." And then he went back the way he had come.

The man left behind opened the driver's door, switched on the ignition, and with an elongated z-shaped lever cranked the engine, which came alive with a roar. The lever started spinning wildly, but the man snatched it out deftly and got into the driver's seat. Before long, the car was chugging down the road; its destination was a small town, Kharkhoda, some twenty-five miles out of Delhi.

Shops and houses receded into the background as it left behind Delhi. The car passed a small church, and further up — more than halfway to its destination — villages surrounded by lush fields, populated mainly by people of the *Jat* Hindu caste.

Outside a small greyish blue *mandir* — a temple dedicated to the Hindu god *Karttikeya*, the driver stopped the car, got out and stretched. The clang of the temple bell reverberated in the air. Seeing a priest, the driver asked him for a drink of water. He downed the glassful the priest brought, and thanked him, then taking a can from the boot of the car poured some petrol into the tank. Leaving behind the strong, sweet smell of benzene mingling with the musky incense, the driver was en-route again.

An hour later, the car arrived at the small town of Kharkhoda. There were not many people on the street, so the driver stopped at a tiny grocery store in front of which, on a verandah a wizened old man lay on a *charpoy*, smoking a *hookah*. The driver leaned out of the car to greet him; "*Babaji*, where does Meer Meherbaan Ali *sahib* live?" he asked him. The old man raised himself on his elbow to scrutinise the car and its driver with narrowed eyes.

"Where have you come from?" he said eventually.

"From Delhi," the driver said.

"Oh, yes? In *that?*" the old man looked disparagingly at the black car in front of him.

"Err, yes…" the driver wasn't sure how to answer that. "I…yes, in this car."

"From whose house?"

"From the house of Justice Khwaja Mehmood Hosain."

"And who is Justice Khwaja Mehmood Hosain?"

The driver groaned, realising this could go on for a while.

"Justice *Sahib's* daughter Riffat Bano is married to Meer Meherbaan Ali *Sahib's* son Syed Sharif Ahmad. Meer Meherbaan Ali *Sahib* lives somewhere here. I would like to know where his house is if you will tell me, please," he said, making an effort to stay polite.

"Gurgle, glug, gurgle," went the *hookah* before its owner spoke again.

"You haven't been here before?"

The driver closed his eyes briefly and muttered something under his breath before saying, "*Babaji*, I'm new to the job."

The old man appeared to be debating the matter. He took another puff at the *hookah*, indulged in a prolonged fit of coughing and then only did he respond with gestures alone: down the road and a turn to the right.

The driver breathed a sigh of relief, thanked the old man and drove off in the direction indicated. "I hope he's right."

He was. Before the car had gone too far down the bumpy road, there came a turn to the right, and within a couple of minutes, it arrived at a large iron gate. As the driver stepped out of his car, a little boy darted out from behind the bushes.

"Is this Meer Meherbaan Ali *Sahib's* house?" the driver asked.

The child nodded breathlessly, staring at the car with his mouth open as the driver swivelled into the driveway, which curved left in a 'D' around a small garden. The driver parked near the entrance of the large house. Carrying the basket, he walked to the carved front door in the shade of a porch, knocked, and looked around while waiting for a response.

The rambling old house was yellow with age. There was a large garden to its left, a smaller one to the right and another house beside that. A walkway joined the two houses. The top floor was set back to leave a spacious balcony, edged with an ornamental cement parapet hung with colourful bougainvillaea. Upturned clay urns covered the roofs of both houses as insulation against the heat.

There were sturdy pillars at the corners of the house, and on the side facing the large garden a deep verandah, almost hidden by a green trellis and jasmine creepers.

The front door opened as a young man hurried out, an older man and a woman close behind him.

"*Salam Sahib*," said the driver. "Judge *Sahib* sent me. Are you ...?"

"Yes, yes I'm Sharif Ahmad," said the younger man, and gesturing behind him, "my father, Meer Meherbaan Ali. Is everything all right?"

"*Ji Sahib, Alhamdulillah*, it's a boy," said the driver. "Riffat *Sahiba* and the little *sahib* are well." He held out the basket with a respectful bow. "*Mubarak, Sahib. Bari Begum Sahiba* and Judge *Sahib* asked me to give you this with their *salaams* and congratulations."

A man came forward to take the basket.

"*Allah ka shukr*," the younger man said, rather shakily, before he was engulfed in an embrace by his parents.

When the older man broke away from his son, he thundered in a firm voice to no one in particular, "Syed Sardar Ahmad. My grandson!" It was apparent he simply wanted to savour the words, "May *Allah's* blessings surround the boy."

Meer Meherbaan Ali looked around to where some of his employees were standing in the doorway, agog for news. "*Meethay chawal,*" he cried in ringing tones. Sweet rice. "Distribute it to everyone in the village and send enough for a hundred mouths to the mosque as well." He turned to one of the men and asked him to make the driver comfortable.

He smiled and patted his son on the back, "Well, young man. You are now a father. *Alhamdulillah.*" *Allah* be praised. "May Allah enhance your life with the birth of your son, may He give the young man strength of mind and heart, and bless him with happiness."

"Amen," Syed Sharif Ahmad said fervently.

"My grandson will be my pupil. I will pass on to him the wealth of wisdom that comes from experience. It will be up to you to pass on to him the wealth of this land."

Sharif Ahmad laughed. "Thank you, *Abba Jan.* It eases my mind, knowing that he has you for his mentor." He accompanied his parents into the house, his father's arm around his shoulder.

24th September, 2016

Syed Sardar Ahmad:

"We were five brothers and no sister. Mukhtar Ahmad was a year younger than me, and Salar Ahmad was one and a half years younger than Mukhtar. Then it was Iftikhar Ahmad, and Waqar

Ahmad was the youngest.

In 1932 when I was five years old, I started going to school in Kharkhoda. It was called Kharkhoda Middle School. It was a model school which meant that English was taught there. I was there until grade five.

There were extra-curricular activities in this school, such as plays, poetry, etc.

Kharkhoda was a town of fifteen to seventeen thousand people. Muslims composed most of the population. There were Hindus as well as scheduled castes. There were no Brahmins in our area. We used to interact freely with the local Hindus, and there was no animosity between us. They used to send us trays full of sweets on Diwali, and we used to send them sheer khorma on Eid. So, our relations with them were harmonious. The only tension was with the Jats in the surrounding villages over the sacrifice of cows.

One of my Hindu friends was Lala Lalli, and there was also Lala Binarsi. There must have been others, but I don't remember their names. Financially the people were doing well.

They were happy.

Performance of the Ramlila — a drama about Ram, Sita, Ravan, and Lakshman — was held every year, usually in September for almost a week. It used to start around 4 p.m. and end by 6 or 7 p.m. Our model school used to have grounds for cricket and hockey, and next to them was a farm where they used to teach us farming. The Ramlila used to take place on those grounds. The performers were from our town. Our master Chandan Lal, he used to participate in as well. The event was free for everyone since it was a religious play. Muslims used to go too. Since the Hindus from our Qasba were the organisers, they would show respect to the Muslims and help them get seated. There were food stalls set up.

The actors used loudspeakers. Kharkhoda did not have electricity till 1947, so the loudspeakers were operated by batteries.**"**

The dusty old road from Sharif Ahmad's father's house led straight to the local Model School where every year, in September, the *Ramlila* was to take place. Large groups of villagers, students, teachers, their families and friends walked up to the school to see the play.

Sardar Ahmad was accompanied by his friends Lalli and Binarsi who lived close to Sardar's house.

The walk would have taken ten minutes for an adult, but it took almost thrice as long for the boys because, of course, there were diversions.

"A *chakri*! Look!" Lalli pounced excitedly on a round red and yellow disc half-buried in the dust. They took turns to play with it, but they didn't have the patience to put it back when the string came away. Instead, they raced to see who would first reach an old grey donkey in a field beside the road. Binarsi won.

"Oh, this donkey is hurt," he said, bending to inspect a wound in the donkey's mouth. The donkey blinked its long-lashed eyes dolefully at the boy.

"Yes, I know," said Sardar. "Its harness was not well-made, and it hurt him, my father told me. He has had a new one made, but they're not going to use it until the wound heals. The man who looks after him cleans the cut every day with saltwater."

Binarsi realised he had lost some coins from his pocket while running, and they had to retrace their steps to look for them.

"Here's one," Sardar said, picking up a large silver coin that had rolled under a stone. The coin had a profile of George VI, the man referred to as the King-Emperor of India wearing a crown on one side.

"One *rupaiya*!" Sardar said. "Why are you carrying so much money?" Before Binarsi had a chance to reply, Sardar had moved on to investigate a hole in a tree and was eager to investigate it. His friends hoisted him up so he could reach it.

"Hurry up! You're as heavy as a horse!" said Lalli with a groan.

"Careful" said Binarsi. "There might be a snake in there." To Sardar's disappointment, the hole was too dark to see what was inside, and he thought better of sticking his hand into it to find out. "It has to be a snake," Binarsi said. "They like to eat birds' eggs, so it's living near them."

"It may be a squirrel," said Sardar. "They live on trees."

"But do they live in holes?" said Lalli. "They make nests and line them with sticks and grass and things. My uncle showed me in a book."

They argued about this until they arrived at the unsteady gate of the long, low building that was the Kharkhoda Model School.

The school grounds were not what they normally looked like. They had erected a large stage in the fields, and the space facing the stage was lined with chairs, ready to be occupied by the audience.

"My father says people should not walk over the playing fields,"

Lalli, the avid hockey player said, anxiously. "I hope we can still play hockey after this."

"I'm sure we can," said Sardar. "They have the play here every year, and we still play hockey, don't we? Look, they've put ropes around the goals to stop us walking on the striking circles, see?" he pointed to where somebody had indeed cordoned off those spaces.

"Look! There's *Babu*!" laughed Binarsi. *Babu* was their Principal's dog. When it spotted the boys, it trotted over with its tail wagging.

With Babu frisking around their legs Sardar and his friends stroll around the fields, which were divided into tiny plots planted with different crops in various stages of cultivation. They were taught farming here, and they wanted to see how their particular patches were doing.

"Look!" Binarsi pointed to some small green plants with straw-coloured grain hanging off the green. "Our rice is almost ready to harvest! *Masterji* says we will cut it when about eighty-five percent of the grain is yellow!"

They inspected the rice and other crops with interest. By this time, almost all the other students and their families had arrived. Boys darted about greeting their friends as *Babu* lolloped around them, barking excitedly. Suddenly the noise was drowned out by the sound of drums and music.

"It's starting! Hurry! Sit down!" The voices were heard from all sides as the children rushed to find places. "Sit down!"

After the inevitable jostling, Sardar and five of his friends settled down right in front of the stage. *Babu* settled himself not far away, his tail raising little clouds of dust as it thumped on the ground. A while later, Sardar's brothers Mukhtar and Salar came to sit behind their older brother and his friends. Mukhtar was a year younger than Sardar, and Salar a year and a half younger than Mukhtar.

Salar tapped Sardar excitedly on the shoulder. "*Bhai*! We're here! We're here, *Bhai*! Behind you! *Apajan* and *Abba Jan* and *Ayah Ji* and Iftikhar are here as well!" Salar said, rambling with excitement.

"Yes, Salar, I see you," Sardar said. "Now be quiet when the play starts, all right?"

He turned to scan the seats for his parents and spotted them, his father wearing his usual *kurta* and *chouridaar pyjama*, his mother a blue cotton *sari*. His mother was carrying their youngest brother Iftikhar. Sardar and his brothers called their mother *Apajan*. When Sardar turned, she waved and spoke to another woman beside her, their *ayah*, and pointed him out to her. A minute later, the *ayah*, holding Iftikhar, came over to sit with the boys.

The actors in costume, mostly their fellow students, were already singing and dancing on the stage.

"That's him! That's him!" squeaked one of Sardar's friends sitting nearby.

"Who?"

"Master Chandan Lal! Look!" the boy gestured excitedly towards one of the adult actors who was wearing no shirt and orange shorts with an ornate gold belt. On his head was a large gold crown shaped like a fan.

"He's Rama!" cried Binarsi.

"Last year, our poetry teacher played Rama, didn't he?" said another boy. "Look! Master's waving at us!".

Just then one loudspeaker died with a sputtering cough. A man jumped onto the stage and changed the loudspeaker's batteries while the actors carried on with their performance. When the loudspeaker came back to life with a boom, the audience covered its ears and burst out laughing.

"My aunt is on the stage, too!" said Binarsi. "See? There! *Massi*! *Massi*!" he exclaimed to a young woman in a bright yellow sari, with a great deal of jewellery in her hair, who waved back happily.

It was a fun sort of play. People from the audience jumped onto the stage and sang and danced with the performers whenever they wished. People brought back *chaat* from the food stalls to eat while watching the performance. The scent of chopped guava hung in the air.

Three hours later, Sardar and his family walked home, along the same road that the car from Delhi had driven through years ago. Nothing much had changed. The old man with the *hookah*, more wizened and now with fewer teeth, still lay on his *charpoy* outside the grocery store, still smoking a *hookah*. He raised his hand to the family as they passed, "*Namaste* Ahmad *sahib.*"

"*Khairiat say ho baba?*" responded Sardar's father inquiring about the old man's health.

"*Ram ki kripa hai,*" he replied. "My legs bother me, so I didn't go to…" he nodded towards the school.

They carried on up the road, turned right and entered their gate. There were balls and a tricycle in the garden, and a couple of hockey sticks propped up against a tree. A rope swing with a plank seat hung from the branches of another tree. The children's grandparents, older and greyer now, sat on chairs near that tree. Rattan blinds all along the verandah were rolled up. In the afternoons, when the sun was at its highest and its rays threatened to enter the house, those blinds were let down covering the verandah completely to keep the house behind it dark and cool.

Sardar joined his grandparents, who were drinking refreshing *lassi*. Their grandmother fussed over the boys because their clothes were covered with grass stains and dirt.

"Couldn't you have chosen a cleaner spot?" she scolded, brushing vigorously at the back of Mukhtar's *kurta*.

"Sardar and his friends were sitting there too," Mukhtar protested.

After a while, Sardar went indoors with his parents, the *ayah* and little Iftikhar, while Mukhtar and Salar stayed back in the garden.

"What did you both think of the play?" asked their grandfather.

"It was a lot of fun, *Dadajan!*" Mukhtar said excitedly. "Rama jumped and danced and sang! The *amrood ki chaat* was so good!" he smacked his lips. "I had two platefuls!"

"And the drums!" cried Salar. "They were so loud! They hit me here!" he patted the centre of his stomach.

"Where? Here?" Meer Meherbaan Ali tickled his little grandson's tummy, and Salar squirmed and giggled.

"Or here?" *Dadajan* tickled Salar's side, and Salar fell across his grandfather's lap, laughing helplessly. His grandfather laughed as well and hugged him. "Such a little frog! Why are you so ticklish?"

"Iftikhar is even more ticklish," Mukhtar said. He looked around. "Did *Ayah* take him inside?"

"Yes," his grandmother said. "It's his bedtime." She stroked Mukhtar's hair away from his forehead. "You have school tomorrow, *beta*. It's time for you to bathe and get ready for bed."

"No-ooo!" wailed Mukhtar. "I'm not sleepy at all! Why must we have all these fixed timings for this and for that?" However, when the *ayah* arrived a few minutes later to take the boys in, he allowed himself to be led away.

26th September, 2016

Syed Sardar Ahmad:

"I remember this piece of poetry from school:

Ghanghor ghata tuli khari thi

Par boondh abhi nahi pari thi

22

Har qatrey ke dil mey tha yeh khatra

Naa-cheez hoon maen ghareeb qatra

I don't remember the rest. I just remember it means that where one drop of rain summons courage to fall, eventually more drops follow, and then it rains. This was during the British Raj, so basically, the message the poet wanted to convey was about the struggle and unity required to be independent and free of our colonial masters. We also read good books like Prem Chand's short stories and Akbar Allahabadi's poetry. I will tell you something interesting: the teachers used to teach students voluntarily for at least a month before middle and matriculation exams. There was no tuition culture then.

We used takhtis, — slates, till grade four. They were readily available to use in the market. There was also another sort of takhti known as Multani; first, we had to wash this takhti and then we could use it, to learn better handwriting. A sarkhanda (reed) was used as the qalam or pen.

My mother was very interested in education, and a great advocate of it. I remember everything about my mother, everything. She prayed five times a day. She never missed a roza. She would pray a lot in Ramadan. She kept telling us, children...her sons...that we should get educated. She would say, 'Property has no value, what is valuable is knowledge. Education brings civilisation; civilisation grows out of education, so my children will get the best education.' She wasn't very educated herself, but in those days a high-quality Urdu literary magazine called Humayun was published from Lahore. Its editor was Mian Bashir. It was an excellent magazine, and my mother used to read it. She used to read books too and was a big admirer of Sir Syed Ahmad Khan because he played a significant role in educating Muslims. She had Mukhtar, Salar and me admitted to Aligarh sometime around 1940, so we transferred out of Kharkhoda Model School.**"**

Sardar's cousins came over a few days after *Ramlila*. They played blind man's bluff, took turns to ride bikes, kicked a ball around and played *pithoo*. When they got tired of knocking down the pile of stones, they built a little city in the corner of the garden.

One cousin, a year younger than Sardar, sat back on his heels to survey the foot-high mud building he had just built. "This is a fort," he said, looking proudly at his handiwork. "People can shoot arrows at their enemies from this tower here," he presented a precariously tapering structure. "Zing! Zing!" He directed twigs and tiny stones from the fort, shooting down imaginary soldiers.

"No one uses arrows now," scoffed Sardar.

"Well, cannonballs then!" said his cousin. "Here comes one! Watch out!" He picked up a small, unripe pear from the ground, and threw it at Sardar.

The pear got Sardar on the nose but although his nose hurt and his eyes watered, "It can't hurt me," he said, spreading out his arms. "I'm big and strong! I'm a…a…warrior…yahhh!" he rolled his eyes and shuffled towards his cousin.

Once his cousins had left, and he was indoors with his parents, lying on the carpet directly under the long-stemmed fan in the living room sporting a cut on his leg, a bruise on his nose and a sore spot on his elbow.

It was a large room. Several recessed doors gave onto the verandah. High above each door was a ventilator, a narrow flap-like window that pulled open or shut using strings that dangled down from the top and bottom of the flap. They were all open now to let the hot air out. The room was full of the scent of jasmine flowers, the last of the season, placed in bowls on the tables.

"I am tired," Sardar yawned and then scowled, thinking of the hockey game he lost to his cousins earlier. "I'll win when they come next time."

"I'm tired too," his mother yawned as well. She was expecting another child soon and was easily fatigued. "Have you done your homework, *beta*?"

"No, but I can't do it now, *Apajan*," pleaded Sardar. "They made me run all around the garden, and it was hot. I feel like melting into a puddle all over the floor. I'll show them," he said again, darkly. "They'd better watch out."

"Mr Chandan Lal will ask you tomorrow if you have learnt your poem," his mother warned, pulling her *dupatta* over her head to offer her prayers.

"He might make you run all around the playing fields if you don't know the poem, and it would be a well-deserved punishment," his father said. "You had plenty of time to learn it."

Sardar had a sudden memory of his teacher in costume and grinned. "It was funny seeing Master Chandan Lal in those clothes at *Ramlila*," he said.

"That's because they belong to the olden days, and you're not used to them," his father said, stretching out his legs and yawning. "People those days would find your *kurta pyjama* just as funny. Come on now and say the poem with me, the one you're supposed to learn. Let's see how much you remember."

Sardar sighed and went to stand in front of his father, his hands clasped behind him, the way he had been taught to stand when reciting something. He winced as his sore elbow touched his back.

"*Gangata khari hui thi….*" he began.

"*Ghanghor ghata tuli khari thi,*" his father corrected him. "The rain was poised and ready."

"*Par boondh abhi nahi giri thi…*"

"*Abhi nahi pari thi,*" his father corrected him again. "But not a single drop had come down as yet."

"*Giri thi, pari thi*, where's the difference?" grumbled Sardar.

"There is a difference. You will learn it if you take an interest in what you are saying."

Sardar tried again and once again tripped over the words.

Sardar's father sighed. "Look, *beta*, this is a special poem. Do you know what it refers to?"

Sardar shook his head guiltily. "No, *Abba Jan.*"

His father glared at him for a moment, then sighed again. "Fine. Go to bed. I can see you're tired. We'll talk about this tomorrow."

Sardar left the room quickly before his father could change his mind.

"They teach them how to stand to attention but not to understand what things mean," Sharif Ahmad muttered under his breath. "Little mimicking parrots."

"You're very right, Sardar *kay Abba*," said his wife with a sigh, but she sounded a little pleased as if she had been waiting for her husband to say this very thing. "I am not happy with the school here either. They get the children to memorise everything, like parrots, as you say. And that dirty matting they sit on in class…" she shuddered.

"There's nothing wrong with that," her husband said a little defensively. "I studied on that matting too, and I managed."

She smiled. "Stop being modest! You've more than 'managed' as you call it. You're knowledgeable, and you teach our children so beautifully. I know that you, like me, want even better for our children. I want the boys to learn English as well as Urdu," she said and went on hurriedly before her husband could say anything. "I never learnt English, and there are so many things I don't understand. I don't want that to happen to my children. I…I want them to study in Aligarh, Sharif Ahmad."

"Aligarh!" exclaimed Sharif Ahmad. He stared at his wife. "Riffat *Begum*, do you realise how far away that is! It takes almost an entire day to get there, and they'll be all…"

"They *won't* be all alone," his wife said firmly, seeing a chink in the cloud. "*Bhaijan* Manzoor Hosain is Head of the English Department at Aligarh as you know. He will see to them." Dismissing the discussion on that conclusive note, she picked up *Humayun*, the Urdu literary magazine she liked to read.

Her husband opened his mouth to respond, and then seemed to decide against it.

"What are you reading?" he took the magazine from her hands. "*Khuda ki dain.* — The Gift of God, 'More than half the night had passed, the city of Muzaffarabad slept in fearsome dark silence.' What is it about?"

"I don't know. I'm about to find out. It's by Khawaja Ghulam-us-Saiyedin of Aligarh," she added pointedly. "Now please make sure that your eldest is in bed where he should be, and not playing with his brothers. I'm too tired to go check on them."

The next evening Sardar's father asked Sardar to come for a walk with him. Mukhtar and Salar came along too, and Sharif Ahmad carried Iftikhar on his shoulders.

"Can we stay and watch the wheat being harvested?" asked

Mukhtar.

"Not right now," his father said. "This is just a quick walk. Salar, step out of that mud hole right now!" he called sternly.

Salar reluctantly did as told with one final splash in a puddle of rainwater and sloshed along behind his father.

It was warm and very humid because of the monsoons. By the time they reached a field behind the house, they were all sweating. There, while the younger boys ran off to play, Sardar's father climbed a small mound, one of many from where he surveyed the state of his fields.

"Come up here," he called his eldest son. When Sardar obeyed and stood beside him, he said, "Take a good look around you and tell me what you see."

Sardar turned in a slow circle, following the direction of his father's finger. He saw the wall surrounding their sprawling yellow house, and the path they had taken to get here, the trees lining it, and behind them a drain to carry away the plentiful rainwater. Off in the distance were more fields planted with gram, wheat, and other crops. Men worked in them with their dhotis tucked up. In the paths between the fields, donkey carts stood laden with produce, soil and tools. There, too, was the deep hole he and his friend Lalli had dug trying to get to the other end of the world, before changing their minds and filling it with water to splash in. He wasn't sure which of these his father was asking him about. He picked one of these things at random.

"I see our...our lands," he said hesitantly.

"And what lies beyond them?"

"*Dadajan's* lands, *chacha's* lands, *chacha's* house, and..." Sardar squinted in concentration, "Your *dadajan's* house and...and ...err...I don't...more land?"

"Yes. More land belonging to people we don't know, other

Indians. Is that right?" Sardar's father said.

"Yes," Sardar said.

"But who is ruling us all?"

"The....the *angraiz*?" said Sardar warily. "King George? The man on the coins?"

"That's right." Sharif Ahmad said. "Well, then." He turned to locate his other sons and spotting them raised his voice. "Come on, boys; we're going home."

When they were back home, and the younger boys had gone to bed, Sardar's father sat him down in the verandah on a stool right in front of him. Riffat Bano was there as well.

"The poem you were supposed to learn yesterday but did not," he let the emphasis on 'not' sink in and succeeded, judging by his son's guilty expression. "It is about all that land around you. You saw on the mound today the vast expansive land that is around us."

"It was about this land?" said Sardar puzzled.

Sardar's father nodded. "About this land, and the land that is beyond this; it is about our homeland, about the whole of India, and the people who own it; and the people who forcibly rule it — and about what needs to be done about that situation."

"But that poem is about water, and drops," protested Sardar.

"It is. When lots of drops of water collected in that ditch you dug with Lalli, what did it become? What can many drops of water make together, Sardar?"

"A puddle? A pond?" Sardar shrugged. "Waterhole?"

Sharif nodded. "All of that! When these drops of water fall together from the sky, they make rain. Sometimes it rains so hard it can wash things away. You remember what happened last year?"

"You mean when the rain flooded those planks right out of our garden onto the road?" said Sardar. "Yes. I remember. Uncle's car hit a plank in the dark, and he hit his head hard on the dashboard," he said enthusiastically.

"Yes," his father smiled, "Exactly that." Then he quoted.

"Ghanghor ghata tuli khari thi

Par boondh abhi nahi pari thi

Har qatrey ke dil may tha yeh khatra

Naa-cheez hoon main gharib qatra

This poem is by Ismael Meerathi, and it is called '*Baarish ka pehla qatra*', Sardar. The first drop of rain is important. It says that although the clouds had gathered, not a drop of rain fell because each drop felt it was nothing more than one mere drop of water. When one single drop of water summons courage to go first, eventually more drops follow, and they actualise their power as they pour down together.

Qatron hi say ho-gi nahar jaari — It is those many drops that form the stream

Chal niklengi kashtian tumhari — That will get your boats moving on their way

Every poem has a message. Do you understand the message this poem gives us?"

Sardar shook his head but tried to look intelligent, making his father laugh.

"The message is about the courage we need to be free. Courage and unity go hand in hand in this struggle for freedom; to remain free and strong is the right of every man and woman. That rain last year, although it was only drops of water, when they came down together they were so strong that they washed away those heavy planks of wood, isn't that right? The poet is referring to our situation with the *angraiz*, he is telling us that we need to work together if we want to free ourselves from our foreign rulers."

He nodded at the look on his son's face, which was like a glass being slowly filled with water. "Good. I want you to remember this meaning well and think about it. Remember that in unity lies strength. Great strength. It goes on to say

> *Qaum ki khabar lo* — Get together with the people.

> *Qatron ka sa ittefaq kar lo* — Come together like those drops of water

Now, go memorise those lines and write them on your *takhti* for me," dismissing Sardar to contemplate this on his own, "And when you get it right, I want you to wash your *Multani takhti* and write the poem on that in your best writing and show it to your *Masterji*. Is that understood?"

"Yes, *Abba Jan*," said Sardar. This conversation had stirred something in him, but he could still not help looking longingly at the hockey sticks propped against the tree as he walked to the door.

"And make sure you sharpen your *qalam* well," Sharif called out, and Sardar raised his hand to show he had heard.

"He's not interested enough," said Sharif to his wife, watching his son walk away dragging his feet.

"He is young," Sardar's mother said consolingly. "You can't expect him to take such matters to heart as much as you do, not yet. You've explained it very well. It will come back to him later when it needs to."

"Yes, but we need it to rain now," said Sharif quietly.

28th September, 2016

Syed Sardar Ahmad:

"There was an admission test for Aligarh school in English. There, the education was in English after Grade 4. I was not good at English because back in our old school the primary mode of instruction was Urdu.

Apart from English, I lagged behind in History and Geography. At Aligarh, they said they would not take me in Grade 6; I would need to repeat Grade 5.

I did my matriculation from Aligarh University's high school and then enrolled in F.Com. to study commerce.

To get to Aligarh from Kharkhoda, a complete day was spent travelling. A bus or a *tonga* took us from Kharkhoda to the Sonipat railway station. Sonipat was around 10 miles from Kharkhoda. It used to take one and a half hours for a *tonga* to reach the station, and there we waited for the train that would take us to Delhi. So, that was maybe two hours of wait at the station, and another one and half hour journey to Delhi. There again we had to wait for the train to Aligarh. From Delhi, a branch of the East India Railway took us to Aligarh.

I don't remember the fare, but what I do remember is that the total monthly expense during my stay at Aligarh was 150 rupees, or maybe less than that. It was very cheap in those days.

Aligarh University was very big. It was located outside the city and was built on a total area of over 1100 acres. In Aligarh, our rooms were cleaned by the house service department. They did the laundry for us, but we had to pay for it. I coped quite well with the fact that I was away from home... so far away from my family.

For a child, it is easy to learn things fast, and I did. It took me just six months to learn English. Most people in Bombay and Madras could speak English well. Even today in India the most understood languages are Urdu and Hindi.**"**

Students in Aligarh were usually from Uttar Pradesh and Jammu, but there were many Bengalis as well. Name any city, and you could find a student from there in Aligarh.

Breakfast, lunch and dinner were taken in the Dining Hall. There was no particular dress etiquette for the dining room. For breakfast and lunch, we would go in our uniforms. You did not wear *sherwanis* to the hall at night.

The food in the hostel wasn't good, but it was available in sufficient quantity. At times *shahi tukra* or chicken was available too, but they were quite tasteless.

The commencement of World War II overshadowed Sardar's birthday in October. It triggered tensions in India as well, close to a snapping point.

"Just how much more can this country take?" *Dadajan* said at breakfast one day. He pushed his *paratha* away fretfully. "The next thing these *angraiz* will expect is for us to fight Germany for them. What do we even know about Germany except that it has a *chughad* — a fool with a strange moustache lifting his arm up and down and speaking a language we don't

33

understand? They have this army called the Wehr…wehrmakht…Wehrmacht . I can't even get my tongue to pronounce it. With this motorised and powerful army, the Germans have already conquered Poland, and what do we possess? A few horses and donkeys and some little firecracker guns. Yet, can we refuse to join the war? No." He thumped his fist on the table. "We'll never survive this."

"Really, *Abba Jan*," said Sardar's youngest uncle with a twinkle in his eye. "You always quote Iqbal's Bal-e-Jibreel,

Kafir hai to shamsheer pay karta hai bharosa,

Momin hai to bay-taigh bhi larta hai sipahi.

If a man lacks faith, he depends upon swords; if he has faith, he might even fight without weapons.' You mustn't give up hope."

"*Abba Jan*, don't worry," Sharif Ahmad said, glaring at his brother, "they've said the Indian Army would not be asked to fight."

Sardar's uncle grunted but did not contradict his brother; instead, he changed the subject.

"You're growing like an elastic band," he said to Sardar.

Sardar was by then a well-grown boy with thick black hair curling crisply around his ears. When his uncle spoke to him, he scowled, because his uncle had spoken in English. Sardar, whose English was rudimentary, was not sure what he'd said, and he didn't like that.

His uncle understood. "I said you're stretching upwards, like this," he said, this time in Urdu. He pulled out an elastic band from his pocket and stretched it — a bit too hard because it broke. He laughed. "Well, you must stop growing before that happens," he messed up Sardar's hair, "And you should learn a bit more English before you move to that new school,

Sardar. They teach in English at Aligarh school after Grade 4, not in Urdu like here."

Sardar scowled even harder, and this time it was because he didn't like being reminded about leaving his school in Kharkhoda for the one in Aligarh.

Sardar's mother had her wish. Before their holidays started at the end of Grade 5, their father took Sardar, Mukhtar and Salar to Aligarh school for admission tests. If they passed and were accepted, they were to start school in Aligarh the following year.

Learning English would be easy, Sardar told himself. He was a quick learner. What he did not like was being forced to put himself through the trouble, but most of all, he dreaded the idea of leaving his old school and friends behind. There was nothing he could do about either of these things though, except hope his parents would change their minds, which did not seem likely.

Going to Aligarh was a daunting journey. It took almost the entire day. Sardar had been away from Kharkhoda only a couple of times before to attend family weddings and functions in nearby towns. The last such trip had been to Rohtak, just twenty miles from Kharkhoda. Then, Sardar's parents had got into a *tonga* with the two youngest children. The older boys, along with Sabir Ali — one of their *khadims* who had been with the family since before Sardar was born, got into a second *tonga*. That entire journey had not taken very long. However, this journey to Aligarh was an ordeal that dragged over hours.

Their father helped Salar up the steps into the bus. Mukhtar and Sardar jumped in. Sharif Ahmad bought four tickets and told them about Sonipat on the way, how it was even nearer the Yamuna River than Kharkhoda, and how the Yamuna was changing its course gradually.

"There's a beautiful tomb in Sonipat, in the middle of gardens," he told them. "It belongs to Khawaja Khizr who lived four or five hundred years ago."

With a look of deep concentration, Salar asked the question most important to him, "Was that before I was born?" he said.

"A little before," replied their father with a smile.

Their father bought tickets for them all when they got to Sonipat station, and they went in. There was a wait of almost two hours for the train. The boys had never been on a train before and were excited about finally taking a ride on one. The long wait taxed their patience.

"Why isn't it here yet?" they kept asking until their father took them to the Station Office to divert their attention.

"Look at this," he said, leading them to a window through which they could see a table on which a large box was lying — the likes of which the boys had never seen before. It seemed to be made of metal and was about two feet wide and almost as deep, with strange black squares on its surface. A man sitting at the desk was tapping on the squares with his fingers.

"What do you think that is?" their father said.

"Is that a...umm?" Sardar excitedly tried to make an intelligent guess but failed to come up with anything.

It was Mukhtar who guessed right. "I've seen a picture of one of those," he said. He screwed up his forehead, trying to remember. "I can't remember where, but people write with it."

"You're right, Mukhtar," his father smiled at him. "This, boys, is a typewriter. You press down on the characters to write what you want to on the paper, so you do not need to use a pen."

They all pressed their noses to the glass, staring. The man's fingers tapped away, and every time he hit a key, a lever was raised, pushing the bar of type against the ink ribbon and on to the paper. His tapping seemed to leave an imprint on the paper, which was wedged into the top of the metal box.

Another man came into the room and then the two men left together.

As the boys stared at the machine in fascination, the train chuffed onto the platform.

Salar wrapped his arms around his father's legs and peeked from behind them at the great, black, smoking locomotive rushing towards them, whistling like an enraged monster.

"Will it run over us?" he cried. His father reassured him it would not.

The train wheezed to a stop beside them, and Sharif Ahmad followed his sons into the train. He had bought tickets to a first-class compartment, which was cooled by blocks of ice under the fan. The children breathed a sigh of relief. The ride to Delhi lasted an hour and a half.

A man wearing a white uniform and a peaked cap stood beside their train. A belt crisscrossed his chest, and a large whistle hung from a cord around his neck.

"That's the guard," Sardar's father said. "When he blows the whistle, people know the train is about to leave. Careful," he added as Salar stumbled down one of the steps. "Would anyone like some water?"

When the boys yelled in unison "Yes!" their father led them to large *matkas* that lined the platforms. They were filled with cool drinking water for the passengers.

Sharif Ahmad checked to find out when the train for Aligarh

would arrive and was told they had to wait an hour for it. To while away the time, he led them out of the station to get a glimpse of Delhi.

They turned to look at the building they were leaving. If they got admission in Aligarh school, this would be their train station. Delhi railway station was red, with arches and turrets edged with white. It was much larger than the railway station at Sonipat.

The street life outside was like nothing the boys had experienced before. There were more cars than they had ever seen; *tongas* trotted on the street, and that interspersed with bullock carts and stray cows. Men on bicycles and a huge crowd of pedestrians could be seen along the road. The clatter of horseshoes on a *pakki* road, horns and bells, men shouting to and at each other, vendors trying to hawk their ware; the noise was overwhelming. A police officer blew his whistle repeatedly trying to direct this mass of humanity so large.

"I would not like to live in all this noise," he told his father, who smiled.

"When your mother first came to Kharkhoda," he said, "she found silence strange and distracting. It is all about what you are used to," he said, smiling at the incredulous expressions on his sons' faces.

A shiny blue car with its hood down drove past them; a man in a *sola topi* was sitting next to a woman in the back seat. The woman's blond hair hung down from under a large brimmed hat

"Who is *that?*" said Mukhtar startled.

"*Abba Jan*, what is wrong with them?" cried Salar, in his high piping voice. "Why do they look like that?"

Sharif Ahmad smiled at his son. "Like what?" he asked.

"Like that!"

"So white! So pink!" said Mukhtar.

Sharif Ahmad laughed. "Well boys, you've seen your first *angraiz*. They were English and that is how they look. The colour of their skin is different from ours. To them, we look just as different."

"Was she the Queen?" said Mukhtar? "Was that the King George VI you often talk about, and say should leave India alone?"

Mukhtar's father's lips quirked again. "No, they live far away, in Great Britain, but these were his countrymen. Mukhtar."

They went back into the station with twenty minutes to spare; while they waited, they had some of the snacks their mother had packed with them.

The East India train arrived with the same puff of smoke and clang as the train to Delhi, but this time they were not scared, and before long they were at Aligarh station.

"Come on, we need to take a *tonga* to the school from here," said Sharif Ahmad. He led them out of the station. The *tongas* were lined up on the other side of the road. They picked one harnessed to a brown horse, with pink and green ribbons tied along its mane and tail. The horse moved its head up and down, its harness jingling, while all four of them climbed up behind it, and then they were off to Aligarh, their new school — maybe.

Sardar never forgot his first sight of Aligarh school with its turrets and minarets, the graceful arches and domes, surrounded by beautiful gardens. The *tonga* drove up to the red building and stopped to let them dismount at the entrance. Sardar had been told that the school grounds covered several acres of land, but he was still not prepared for the beauty and sheer size of everything around them.

Compared to their cosy little school in Kharkhoda, the prospect of living here was intimidating. All three brothers felt the same way.

"I do not want to come to this school," said Mukhtar, firmly, and Salar simply held on to his father's hand and would not let go.

As the eldest, Sardar was used to putting on a brave face and dismissing his brothers' fears, but he could not help agree with Mukhtar this time. Even their father seemed a little nervous. Sardar squared his shoulders and followed his father as briskly as he could, holding Mukhtar's hand in his; together, they walked into the building.

They found themselves in a spacious foyer. The portrait of a man wearing a red Turkish fez hung on the wall in front of them. A long, white beard flowed over the man's chest, and his piercing eyes seemed to bore sternly into each of them as they stood in front of him.

"That's Sir Syed Ahmad Khan," Sardar's father told them, nodding towards the portrait.

The boys stared wide-eyed at the man they had heard so much about.

Their mother had told them that Sir Syed Ahmad Khan had died over forty years ago. "There is a lot of new knowledge in the world, my sons," she had said. "And you need to learn as much of it as you can. You will not understand most of it if you don't learn to read in English. Sir Syed set up Aligarh school for Muslim students so that the Muslims of India would not be left behind in this race for modern knowledge. When you go to Aligarh school, you will be taught modern subjects by good teachers. You will like the school; I know you will."

Right now, though, Sardar's resentment resurfaced as he

stared at the portrait; it was because of this man's ideas that they were there. They would have to leave their friends behind in the Model School in Kharkhoda.

Sardar's stomach had not felt quite right ever since he'd learnt his parents wanted to move him to a different school, and now it positively hurt.

"Chacha's friend was talking about Allama Mashriqi yesterday, but Chacha did not agree with the views of this man at all. I don't even know who Allama Mashriqi is but which of them should I believe?" he had asked his father a few days ago.

"There will always be different opinions on any given subject, Sardar," his father had replied. "You will understand this when you study at your new school. Remember, a difference in opinion does not mean the other person is wrong. Every argument has its strong as well as its weak points."

That answer had not helped settle the confusion in Sardar's mind.

Now that they were at Aligarh, with an entrance exam imminent, their father tried reassuring them, "The most that will happen is that you might fail some subjects and need to repeat a class," he said casually.

Sardar had never failed before, and he did not want to fail now, so he walked into the large, cool hall for his exam with gritted teeth.

There were many students in the hall. Sardar heard several languages spoken around him as the students were settled into seats by their parents. Then a bell sounded, the parents filed out, and the students were left facing a teacher on a dais, while other teachers passed out their papers.

The three boys took the exam and then they all left for Delhi, feeling much happier now that the ordeal was behind them. In Delhi, they stayed the night at a hotel, in a suite of rooms named after Razia Sultana.

"Razia Sultana, the daughter of Iltutmish, was the first and only woman to rule over Delhi," their father told them.

The boys were struck by the idea of a female ruler, Mukhtar most of all. "Was she married to a king, or was she a king all by herself?" he asked his father.

"She was a queen, a queen who ruled over Delhi all by herself," he said. "Her husband was Malik Altunia."

The story ended on how the ruling queen was assassinated.

Maybe I'll learn all about such things when I come here, Sardar thought humbly, I didn't know any of this.

They returned home, and a couple of weeks later a letter arrived addressed to *Janab* Sharif Ahmad *sahib*. There was a big round seal at the back which said: 'Aligarh Muslim University,' in English. Around it were the famous words from the Quran: "*Allamal insana malam ya'lam*" He gave man the knowledge which man knew not.

Sardar had passed the entrance exam, the letter told them, as had Mukhtar and Salar. However, his father was right. Sardar was to repeat Grade 5 to give him time to catch up with English.

"Don't be upset," his mother reassured him. "You won't be the only one repeating a class. There will be many boys doing the same. Students come to Aligarh from all over India, and most of them did not have a prior opportunity to learn English."

She was right, yet it was humiliating. Sardar was not only used to putting on a brave face, but he was also used to being looked up to by his siblings. His only comfort was that Mukhtar was also to repeat a year, so there would be no crowing.

The three brothers started school at Aligarh in April 1940. By then, Sardar's grandfather had been proven right. Even though the British had said they would not involve the Indian Army in hostilities, not long after the Second World War started India was asked to join the campaign in North and East Africa, as well as in France.

Sardar's mother packed snacks for her sons to eat on the way. She also packed some things for school, boxes of mulberries which they all loved, packets of raisins, and *channay*. Before they left, she said a special prayer, hugged each of them and asked them to listen carefully to what she had to say.

"Remember this, all three of you: Sardar, Mukhtar, and Salar: You will have the opportunity for a great education at Aligarh. You will *In Sha Allah* learn more than you would have anywhere else. Make the most of it. Believe in the power of knowledge. God has blessed us with all this," she gestured to the house and the expansive span of land, "But property holds no lasting value. What is valuable is what you possess in here," she tapped her oldest son's forehead, "And what you possess in here," she tapped her youngest son's heart. "You take it with you wherever you go. Remember that. Education makes us better human beings. So, as far as you are concerned, education should be your primary focus. May Allah bless you, my sons."

They repeated the long journey from Kharkhoda to Aligarh with their father. The weather was better than it had been when they went there for their tests. There was nervous expectancy, but the journey seemed shorter this time because what lay ahead was no longer as unknown as before.

At the railway station in Delhi now, most of the people in the station were students and their parents, but there were also turbaned men in army uniform on the platform, wearing belts across their waists and straps across their chests. Some of them — when Sardar looked at them closely — were very young despite their impressive moustaches.

The Aligarh station was no different; army jeeps winding their way through the bikes and pedestrians on the street.

"They're going to war," said Sharif Ahmad soberly. "May God be with them."

They took a *tonga* to school, where a sea of students clad in a black *sherwani* with white *pyjama* was milling around the buildings.

"Are there no non-Muslims here?" Sardar asked the boy who showed them around the first day.

"Why do you say that?" he asked. "There are students from all ethnicities and all religions studying here. We even have a Hindu teacher, the one who teaches Commerce. His name is Agarwal. There may be others too. There are quite a few Hindu students in the Engineering College."

Perhaps Lalli and Binarsi will want to be Engineers, Sardar thought desperately. Then they can come here too.

Their father pointed out the two tiny minarets at the entrance, and the graceful arches. "That architecture is your heritage," he said, "you will learn someone else's language, but the knowledge you will acquire belongs to everyone. Make good use of it."

Although their home was well furnished, at school, they had studied on mats on the floor. So, for Sardar and his brothers, the benches and desks at Aligarh were daunting, however comfortable. Finally, Sardar decided to change his perspective on the matter.

"I can push you off your bench if you don't behave yourself," he told Mukhtar, who slid smoothly off the bench and left, poking his tongue out at his brother.

Other than their family and friends, the boys missed the food at home, which was always excellent; the vegetables picked from their fields that very day and delicately prepared just before each meal.

"We get *shahi tukray* and chicken and all sorts of good things here," Sardar wrote home to his parents, "but it's hard to tell one from the other this is how tasteless they are."

"I miss you," Mukhtar wrote simply to his mother.

"Are your rooms comfortable?" their mother asked them in her first letter. "I'm told the cleaning staff is large and efficient, they change your sheets every week, and tidy up."

"We're very comfortable, yes," Sardar reassured her. "We never see our beds being made and the rooms being cleaned, but everything is clean, dusted and ready for us when we come back from classes."

Mukhtar, on the other hand, was not as comfortable. At home, his mother would pick out his laundry and make sure his things were looked after. At school, he kept forgetting to leave his dirty laundry in the right place and leave his shoes for polishing. As a result, his clothes were frequently unwashed and crumpled, and his shoes dusty. He was often in trouble.

With a scowl on his face, Mukhtar wrote a hundred lines as punishment for leaving dirty clothes on the floor. "I'm not sure where his thoughts are," Sardar wrote to his mother, watching Mukhtar in the common room, "But they're not here."

Part II

Syed Sardar Ahmad:

"Aligarh was an institution in itself, a mini Pakistan. No one had the courage to even point a finger at a student of Aligarh in the city. It was very disciplined. We had monitors. I too was one of the monitors at school. To wear a cap, socks and shoes, and carry a handkerchief, this was a must before leaving your room in the hostel. In the cinema, the best seats were given to us at a concession. It was a beautiful environment. There was so much brotherhood because we didn't discriminate among people for being Bengali, Punjabi, Bihari, Gujrati, Balochi, Sindhi or Pathan. There was no sense of who is a Hindu, Sikh or Muslim; there was no conflict between Sunni or Shia either. There was a mosque which was a replica of Delhi's *Jamia* Masjid, where first Sunnis, and then Shias used to pray.

There was a phone, but it was very difficult to place a call. You would have to wait for hours to receive one.

At the railway station in Delhi, there was different food for Hindus, Muslims and Europeans. The food was remarkable, the service was excellent, but the prices varied. In the waiting rooms, there were comfortable chairs to lie down on. Rest houses and waiting rooms had great arrangements.

At the railway station at Sonipat, trains came after long gaps. It was like what we have in our small cities today.**"**

There were several mosques on the school grounds.

"This one is just like the *Jamia Masjid* in Delhi," Mukhtar said, excitedly, when he saw the main University mosque, a red building with white domes and graceful minarets. "I've seen its pictures!"

"Yes, it is," the teacher who was with them at the time confirmed. "You students will be saying your prayers here. There's also another one, called the Sir Syed Mosque which is just like the Badshahi mosque in Lahore. That is in Sir Syed Hall. Sir Syed is buried there. He had both this *Jamia* Mosque and the Sir Syed Mosque built himself."

"Oh!" said Mukhtar in awe.

Every morning the students were woken by a bell and were expected to wash and dress in a clean uniform before leaving the hostel for morning prayers. Shia and Sunni prayed at the same mosque, one after the other.

"I like this uniform," Sardar thought, looking at himself in a mirror in their dormitory. The black *sherwani* that completed the uniform had a monogram with the school motto in Arabic: 'He taught man what man knew not'. Students wore the *sherwani* during the day but were allowed to dress more casually at night for dinner in the hall.

Sardar moved away from the mirror for another boy who wore an Aligarh-cut pyjama instead of a *shalwar*, who also wanted to make sure he looked as he should.

"Come along, there isn't much time," their dorm monitor called, hopping on one foot trying to get his shoe on.

Sardar and Salar got used to the school before long and began to like it very much, but Mukhtar continued to find it difficult to adapt himself to his new surroundings and routine, and the various details involved in their dress code. The boys were supposed to wear a Turkish cap, socks, and black shoes, and to have a clean handkerchief in their pocket at all times. Mukhtar was invariably caught out with yesterday's crumpled handkerchief, or an unwashed *kurta*, his *sherwani* unbuttoned, or buttoned all wrong.

"How am I to remember to do all this!" he almost cried when Sardar tried to explain the best way of folding a pocket square, which was not the way Mukhtar had been doing it. "There just isn't time in the morning."

"But even Salar manages to do these things!"

Mukhtar growled, and Sardar decided to let his brother's dorm monitor deal with the issue.

Sardar himself was made a monitor almost right away; being entrusted with such a responsibility pushed him to do even better.

"I never doubted you would settle in well," his mother wrote to him, which added to his pride.

Within a few weeks, all three boys were well on their way to catching up with their peers.

A few days before the summer holidays which started at the end of May, Sardar was in his dorm taking some books out of his bag for that day's homework when a small boy came into the dorm calling, "Sardar Ahmad! Sardar Ahmad! Is Sardar Ahmad here?"

Sardar's heart thudded within his chest. Had he done something wrong? "I'm here," he said a little too loudly, conscious that the other boys were staring at him.

"You're wanted. Main office. School Secretary. You're in

trouble, ha-ha!" said the little scamp, running away.

It was a vast campus stretching over several acres, and the office was a long way off through several courtyards, down lengthy corridors in a different building altogether.

What had he done? What had happened? Fear gripped Sardar as he ran all the way. He got lost a few times. By the time he arrived at his destination, he had even considered being kicked out of school in disgrace. He knocked at the office door with an unsteady hand.

"Come in," said a firm voice.

Sardar opened the door and walked into the room. The school secretary sat at a desk in his black *sherwani* and fez, talking to a couple of teachers.

"I umm I am Sardar Ahmad," Sardar stammered. "You wanted to s…see me?"

"Ah yes. Sardar Ahmad," said the secretary pleasantly. "Sit down," he gestured to a chair. "Your mother wants to talk to you." He pointed to the Bakelite phone on his desk. "The call will come through here. It will take some time."

Sardar felt almost faint with relief. He was not going to be expelled. He sat back in his chair when it suddenly occurred to him that perhaps something awful had happened at home. Why else would his mother wish to speak to him? He sat up, tense, picturing her worried and restless as she was, waiting for the call at their local post office, the only place in Kharkhoda that had a phone.

His eyes darted from the telephone to the secretary and teachers poring over timetables and letters.

The walls were covered with shelves full of books in warm red and brown covers, many of them in English, others in Urdu or Hindi and a few others in Persian and Arabic.

The phone was still silent. It was 2 p.m; the enormous grandfather clock against a wall signalled the hour with a deep booming sound. A bird outside on the window sill took flight at the sound.

After what seemed like hours but was only twenty minutes, Brrr!!" The phone rang. Sardar jumped and went quickly up to the secretary's desk.

"Hmm. You're lucky, young man. Normally it takes longer," said the secretary. "Hello! Hello!" he shouted, picking up the receiver. "Yes, he is here; he is here." He held the receiver out to Sardar.

"Hello!" Sardar whispered into the receiver. He had never used a phone before.

"You're holding it the wrong way up," one teacher said kindly, "Here," he turned the receiver around for Sardar.

"And talk louder," added the secretary. "They're a long way off and won't hear you if you speak so softly."

So, "Hello!" bellowed Sardar.

"Sardar *beta*, this is *Apajan*," he made out his mother's voice through a buzzing interference. "Can you hear me?"

"Yes! Yes, *Apajan*, I can hear you!" Sardar shouted back, noting with relief that she didn't sound worried. Still, "Is everything all right?" he asked her.

"Yes, all right, all right. *Beta* I will send Sabir Ali to Aligarh. He will meet you at school and bring you three back the day your holidays start. Do you understand?"

"Yes!" Sardar shouted. "Sabir Ali. We'll wait for him."

"Remember to bring all your clothes with you," his mother said. "And make sure to tell your teachers before you leave."

"I will!" Sardar shouted. "We will!"

"Three minutes," broke in the operator's voice and the call ended.

Sardar stayed where he was for a few seconds, stunned. "Thank you," he said eventually. He said *salaam* to the teachers and the secretary and ran off to give Mukhtar and Salar the news, and to tell them he had used a telephone.

"Does it hurt?" implored Salar.

Sardar airily shrugged off the question.

Sabir Ali, a tall man with long moustaches curling upwards, was the familiar sight from Kharkhoda all three boys were happy to see. He arrived early at the school with a *yakka*, a horse cart without seats which left more space for all of them and their bags. He took charge of their cases and slung them in effortlessly. As they all crowded in the cart, it gave a great jolt and began its journey towards the station; the boys fell back over their luggage, rolling in laughter.

Their trip home was full of happy anticipation, in spite of the heat of May. By the time they reached the station, Sardar and his brothers were drenched in sweat.

"Remember that ice in the train?" Mukhtar reminded his brothers longingly.

Sardar grunted. It was going to be a long day.

The train was due to arrive in about an hour and a half. They spent the time in the railway waiting room with Sabir Ali keeping a watchful eye on them.

"These rooms are good," said Sardar, pacing restlessly around the large area, "It's even quite cool here. But I can't stand the wait. There's nothing to *do*!" he whacked the back of an empty bench. The lady on the bench opposite glared at him and muttered something to her husband.

"She's telling him you're a brat," said Mukhtar with a grin. He was stretched out on one of the long deck chairs that dotted the room.

"She's probably talking about her own son," replied Sardar as the toddler on the woman's lap grabbed his mother's ears and jumped up and down on her legs, making her protest.

"It will be fun to see Lalli and Binarsi and the others," Sardar allowed his mind to wander off..

"And my friends!" Salar added fervently.

Sardar beckoned a server.

"Muslim?" the server asked as a preliminary, and when the boys said they were, he selected one of the several menus in his hand and handed it to them. The food on the Muslim menu was *halal*. There were separate menus for Hindus and Christians each as well; the one for Hindus respected their choice to avoid beef.

The boys and Sabir Ali selected some snacks.

When they reached Delhi, there was another wait for the train to Sonipat. They had some *murgh pulao* while waiting for the train. The older boys and Sabir Ali ate hungrily, but Salar found the chicken rather spicy. Sabir Ali got him bananas to eat, the price of which left him grunting about city vendors.

As their train chugged along, they saw some familiar landmarks and knew they were nearing Sonipat.

At Sonipat, Sardar suggested they take a *tonga* instead of a *yakka,* but Sabir Ali turned down the suggestion.

"There will be no space for your bags in a *tonga*," he said firmly. "I'll have to pile them all on your heads."

So, it was dusk when their horse trotted up the street towards their house. The rhythmic movement lulled Sardar to sleep. He awoke with a jolt when the horse stumbled and his gaze fell upon the grocery store in front of which he was used to seeing the old man with his *hookah*. He was not there.

"Where's *Babaji*?" he asked Sabir Ali.

Sabir Ali shrugged. "His son took him away."

"What? Why?" As long as Sardar could remember, the old man had been smoking his *hookah* in this spot greeting passers-by, "Was he sick?"

Sabir Ali shook his head. "He was old but able to look after himself. I heard his son felt there were too many Muslims in this village."

"Too many...?!"

Just then they turned into the gate for their house, and Sardar dropped the conversation when his mother came running out, followed by his brother Iftikhar. The absence of the old man was the first jarring note in Sardar's life. Even as he greeted his family, he felt an unease he had never felt before.

1ˢ October, 2016

Syed Sardar Ahmad:

"Hunting was our major entertainment in Kharkhoda: deer, fowl, partridge and wild geese — teetar murghabi.

The *Jats* in the villages surrounding ours used to tell us not to sacrifice cows. We said we were allowed to by our religion and wouldn't stop. This caused a little tension between us.

You couldn't have a gun without a license there. A hunting license was taken separately.

We used to go hunting during our vacations,

especially in winter. We would never hunt in August-September because this was when the deer used to give birth. Other than that we had our gardens and orchards and we used to go there, eat fruit, and play cricket.

In Aligarh, horse riding was available for junior students but not for the seniors.

Extra-curricular activities were drama, poetry, cricket, hockey, swimming. When it rained, the warden would ask us to go out and play. For entertainment, we had the cinema in the city. There were *yakkas* on which we used to travel to the city. They had no seats, you needed to sit on the floor, and horses would pull the cart.

Indian films were screened at those cinemas: *Jhoola*, and there were others too. Actors like Ashok Kumar and Dilip Kumar were very popular. There were English movies as well, but I don't remember any of them.**"**

Despite the excitement of being home, they slept early that night; they were so tired. The next day, their first real day of holidays, was special. Their mother cooked their favourite dishes for each of them, and their father had a *shikar* party planned. Sardar, Mukhtar and their uncles were to join. Salar would have his friends over while his two elder brothers were out for the hunt.

"You have grown tough and strong, young man," his grandfather said to Sardar at breakfast. He looked sharply at his grandson. "It looks like you get a lot of exercise at that school of yours. What do you do?"

"I ride horses," said Sardar, "and play some cricket."

"I'm better at riding than he is," said Mukhtar, chewing briskly at his *paratha*.

Sardar gave his younger brother a quelling look but admitted he was right. "He can make them canter," he said. "I'm still learning to cope with a trot. Salar managed to get up on his horse for the first time just before we came here."

Mukhtar nodded. "Yes, he went up from one side and fell off the other."

Everyone laughed, even Salar.

"The horses are so much bigger than him," said Sardar with a smile. "You'll grow, Salar, don't worry. Mukhtar here can never remember not to walk behind his horse," he added. "But he will once he has had a taste of his horse's back kick that will land him right back in Kharkhoda."

Mukhtar shrugged. "I haven't been kicked yet," he said, now wiping his plate clean with a piece of *paratha*.

Sardar sighed. "My horse hates me. I might get that kick before you do."

"You just might. My teacher told me animals detect fear and take advantage of it." Mukhtar drained his glass of milk and placed it on the table with a thump. "I'm going out."

After breakfast, when alone with his mother, Sardar told her, "It is funny, *Apajan*, but for everything that Mukhtar does he forgets two other things."

Sardar's mother nodded soberly. "He's always been like that. I'll have to see what to do about it. But I can't think about that now, nor can your father. He's worried enough as it is."

"Why? What about?"

Riffat Bano sighed. "Several things, *beta;* he is most concerned about the raging war that has engulfed our world as well."

Sardar nodded. "Yes. I'm sure he is. I wish they'd keep India out of their war."

His mother nodded with a rueful smile. "I wish they'd keep themselves out of India." She shook her head as if to clear it. "*Khair*, what are you planning to do today?"

Sardar stood up. He had things to do, other than worry about the war "Well, if there's time, I'd like to see Lalli and Binarsi for a while."

His mother bit her lip. "Sardar, Lalli and his family have moved. Didn't he write to tell you?"

Sardar gaped at his mother. "What! No, he didn't tell me! Why…are you sure?"

His mother nodded. "Yes, *beta*, I'm sure. I think it's… maybe his father wanted to be with his brothers and the rest of the family. It happens. They've moved to Jaipur."

"But he didn't tell me!" repeated Sardar, stunned. Lalli was a close friend; his leaving without a word felt like a betrayal. Then he remembered, "It's because there are too many Muslims here, isn't it?" he asked his mother. She said nothing.

Sardar's father asked him what was troubling him when he loaded his gun in almost complete silence during *shikar* that evening, but Sardar just shook his head. He was not ready to talk about how coming back home had unsettled him.

"I like venison very much," his father's youngest brother was saying when Sardar finally caught up with them, "but there is something about a good beef kebab that nothing can beat." He heaved a sigh. "I feel like having one right now."

"Don't talk about beef here," his other brother warned him, softly. "Some of these men are Hindu." With a slight jerk of his head, he indicated the men walking behind them, carrying extra guns, ammunition and water. Later they would help carry those same things back. The game, the deer on a pole, and the venison and partridge all strung together was carried by the Muslims.

Is that why Lalli and his family left, Sardar wondered because they didn't like us eating meat? But they've lived here so long, he reasoned, they've never eaten beef, and we always have. What drove them away now?

"Well Islam allows us to eat beef," Sardar's uncle stated defiantly. "I don't see why we should stop because they don't like it." He refrained from saying anything more when he saw the stern expression on his brother's face.

"I like your gun," he said to his brother. He was good at changing the subject. "May I try it?" Sharif Ahmad handed the gun to him.

The young man weighed it in his hands and took a shot.

"Nice! It seemed almost to lock in on the target." He looked closely at the barrel. "Winchester 12. I might get it."

"The license takes a while to get here," Sardar's father told him. "You know you can't shoot in August and September."

"I know, I know." He ran his finger along the barrel. "I wonder what the Allies using in the war."

Sardar noticed his father's expression change. "It will be something deadlier than this," Sharif Ahmad replied, grimly. "The Germans are not as easily downed as partridge or deer. They make a much more dangerous target. The British are not easy to prey at either," he added.

"That we know," his other brother said, with a mirthless laugh.

Their youngest brother said nothing.

They got a deer, some partridges, and Sardar bagged a black-naped hare. Afterwards, they trooped home, hot and dusty. By the time they had washed and changed, the fowl was almost ready for the table. The deer would be cooked the following day.

The scene was forever engraved in Sardar's mind: his parents, his uncles, along with him and his brothers, waiting for dinner in the verandah, with Sardar's grandparents. Sardar's grandmother reclined against a velvet bolster cushion on a divan, a large silver *paan daan* by her side, spreading lime and catechu paste on *paan* leaves for after dinner. Sardar sat beside her, picking out roasted caraway for himself.

"The standard at Aligarh must be much higher than here in Kharkhoda," Sardar's uncle observed as he sat down by his mother's side. "Are you coping?"

"Yes, it is a lot higher," said Sardar, picking up another pinch of caraway. "*Apajan* and *Abba Jan* were right. A grade 7 student came to Aligarh from another small school like the one in Kharkhoda and was admitted in grade 5 with us. At least I had to repeat just one class. The students from Bombay and Madras find it much easier. They say schools are better there."

"They are, but they vary like everywhere else," his uncle said. "What are you studying in Urdu?"

"Munshi Prem Chand," said Sardar, adding some sweet pieces of misri to the fennel in his hand, "And Akbar Allahabadi's poems, but I like Prem Chand's short stories much more."

His mother smiled, "You always did like Prem Chand. How do you like Meer Amman's 'Bagh-o-Bahar'?"

"Yes, definitely that too," Sardar smiled back at her.

The door opened just then, and a man walked in, a close friend of Sharif Ahmad's who joined them occasionally in the evening. They greeted him. One of the boys pulled up another chair.

"What do you boys do when you're not studying?" said his uncle. "Are there any cinemas near the school?"

"Yes, in the city," said Sardar. "Two or three miles away, so we go there. I've only been to one movie yet, but some of the other boys go quite regularly. They show Dilip Kumar's films and the boys were talking about some Raj Kumar movies they liked last year. Jhoola… Nirmala… Have you seen either of them?"

"Yes, both. Nirmala was good," the uncle said. "That was Ashok Kumar in Nirmila though, not Raj."

"Which one did you see?" Sardar's mother asked her son.

"I saw Miss Frontier Mail," said Sardar. "With the Fearless Nadia." His eyes shone. "She jumped from the top of one train to another, fighting bandits! It was good!"

His mother expressed exasperation.

"*Apajan,* it was terrific! Fearless Nadia picked up some of the bandits and threw them right off the train!"

"I'm sure that was very interesting," *Apajan* said carefully.

"How about English movies?" Sardar's father's friend asked.

"There are those too," Sardar shrugged. Some of my friends like them; they say most of these movies are about cowmen, their horses and their guns."

"I think that's cowboys," his father's friend corrected him.

"Oh yes, cowboys. They're men who…who ride horses and use ropes to catch other horses, and sometimes other people too," Sardar made a rotating movement above his head with his hand. "Well, so there are movies, and we also ride, play games, cricket, swimming…"

"And hockey," piped up Salar, swinging an imaginary stick, "Warden tells us to go and play outside even when it rains . He says it makes us tough."

"He's right. Exercise makes you tough," agreed his grandfather.

"And there's also drama and poetry," offered Mukhtar. "I want to start a poetry club."

"That's a good idea," his grandfather said. "Let's hear your favourite piece."

Mukhtar obliged:

> *'Bay khauf e ghair dil ki agar tarjuman na ho* — If without fear of strangers the tongue cannot truly express the heart

> *Behtar hai iss say yeh keh sirray say zuban na ho* — It would be better if there were no tongue to start with."

"Jauhar!" *Dadajan* seemed surprised, "You like his poetry?" Mukhtar nodded, "Very much." With a grin, he looked directly at his father's friend who was said to indulge now and then:

> *'Karna hi tha haram toh phir waday kis liyay* — If the wine had to be not allowed, then why the promise of wine (in heaven)?

> *Yeh kiya kay mai halal ho wahan yahan na ho* — It isn't fair, that something should be allowed there…and forbidden here."

The company dissolved in laughter. "Oh, your argument exactly!" Sardar's father roared as he gave his friend a hearty slap on the back.

Later, when everyone was enjoying the *shikar* in the dining room, Sardar's uncle complimented the qorma, "Wonderful masala *bhabhi sahib*," he said, smacking his lips appreciatively. "Almonds, yes? And yoghurt?"

"Almonds, yes, but no yoghurt," Sardar's mother laughed. "And no tomatoes either. Try again."

"No yoghurt. Then…Cream?" Sardar's uncle tried again. He was rewarded with a nod and a smile.

"I caught this one," Sardar pointed to a dish on the table. "It was sitting on the peepal tree by the pond."

"I presume it's not venison then," said his father's friend.

"No one can argue a deer cannot sit on a tree," said Mukhtar. "It just can't climb one, right?"

"Well, no one can say a Muslim can't live in peace in India either," quipped the quite uncle, swallowing his mouthful, "He just won't be allowed to."

The deafening silence gave more credence to the remark. Sardar stared around the table, from his father biting his lip to his grandfather glower like winter's icy peak.

"Bring the *sewian*," Sardar's mother broke the silence in a firm voice. The *khidmatgar* brought in the dessert, and forcibly it became the focus of the conversation like nothing else deserved to be discussed more avidly.

Later, when everyone had chewed paan, and his parents had left the room, Sardar's uncle leaned his head back against his chair. "God! Why is *Abba* so averse to discussing the current situation?" he cried in exasperation. "He can carry on for hours about the first famine in Bengal two hundred years ago and what caused it, but refuses to acknowledge what is happening in India these days!"

"*Chacha* is right," muttered Sardar under his breath to Mukhtar. "*Dadajan* likes discussing politics."

Mukhtar said nothing.

"Try and understand him," Sharif Ahmad said wearily. He stood up and began to stride around the room. "Being a landowner is his identity. This talk of new demarcations, of territorial adjustments, of autonomy and independent states. This war, the tussle between the Congress and the League, it threatens life as he knows it. His destiny as Meer Meherbaan Ali, is that of, a *numbardar*, magistrate."

"There are things beyond the status quo, *Bhaijan*," said his brother quietly. "Remember 1857, our *Pardadi Jan* (Great-Grandmother) Naseeb-un-Nissa? She lost everything — her family and her house. When Captain Drake strolled into Kharkhoda, he hunted down even the children of our family, killing our ancestors in cold blood. He spared not one life, he did not spare us our lands, yet here we are, still in Kharkhoda. One lone woman with a baby on the way survived. The bloodline continued, and the ancestral land was returned to the family. We thrive in Kharkhoda today, but what we once lost we might lose again."

"*Allah na karay*! Our family has made sacrifices before; the land our ancestors enriched with cultivation was usurped. Our family was wiped out. Allah was kind, and we survived in spite of the tragedy that befell our family in 1857. If He wills all will be okay," Sharif Ahmad paused as if saying a silent prayer for the safety of his family. He continued, trying to placate his younger brother, "The fact remains that our father is an old man. It gets less easy to change perspective the older you get. Don't forget that he did support the Government of India Act in '35, which changed many things."

Sardar's uncle retorted, "Well, so did I, because it got rid of that 'diarchy' which was an absurd concept, completely unworkable. But now I agree with Jinnah when he calls even the 1935 Act totally unacceptable. Look where it got us," he said. "Congress gets eight of the… what, eleven provinces? And we've seen what happened there. Congress is representing its own interests at the expense of Muslims. If it comes into power one day, we're dead. The Hindu *Mahasabha* is everywhere, the *Vidhya mandir* system in schools for Hindus, Muslims, alike. We ruled this country, only to end up singing the *Vande Matram* and losing our identity. Jinnah even called it the 'Kulturkampf,' like what Hitler is doing in Germany. Is this what we want? The Hindus will do everything to make sure we don't rule them again! I was in Lahore for the *Qarardad*. There were millions of people there. I support autonomy for Muslims."

"Yes, but please don't talk about the Lahore Resolution in front of *Abba Jan* yet," said Sharif Ahmad firmly. "Let him get used to the idea first. What does this 'autonomy' mean, anyway? Is India to be torn apart? What will happen to our lands? To *Abba Jan's* lands? Is India to be divided into separate countries? Our India, the India of our ancestors?"

His brother laughed uproariously, "Our India! Is it really ours, *Bhaijan*? I thought it belonged to the British! The Viceroy brought war upon us last year without batting an eyelid over what we think." He turned to Sardar's father's friend. "Tell me. You're in the Indian army, so when are *you* leaving for the war?"

When the friend said nothing, Sardar's uncle repeated his question. "Go on. Tell us. When are you leaving?"

The man sighed. "Next week."

Amidst the sounds of general concern, Sardar's uncle laughed bitterly, "Well… can you still call India ours? We have a Governor-General, an Englishman, dictating his own terms to us. George the fifth, sixth, seventh, whatever he calls himself sits on his throne miles away and still holds the power to do as he pleases with *our* India. It is *their* parliament that is supreme, *Bhaijan*. The British can suspend our government. They can send us to war; they can leave whomever in charge of India; they can do whatever they like here."

When Sardar's father was about to speak, his brother held up his hand. "What happened to the promises made by the Simon Commission? Didn't the British say they'd give us 'Dominion Status'? But the Act makes no such provision" he ran his hand wearily across his face. "I don't know. They'll work it out, I suppose, I hope, but think about it — maybe this 'Pakistan' that Chaudhry Rahmat Ali spoke of is not such a bad idea."

3rd October, 2016

Syed Sardar Ahmad:

"The population of Kharkhoda was approximately 20,000 people, and it was predominantly Muslim. There were Hindus there too, and some scheduled castes as well. Even in a predominantly Muslim area, there were Hindu temples and also a church.

Within a 12 mile radius, there was one other village besides our's that had a Muslim majority; forty Hindu *Jat* villages surrounded us, and the people in those villages were very influential. There were a handful of Muslim homes in these Hindu villages. They belonged to technicians, ironsmiths or carpenters etc. These artisans were needed there. However, they were not allowed to offer sacrifice on Eid. There was not a single Sikh in our village. At our old school in Kharkhoda, almost 80% of the teachers were Hindu. They did not discriminate between us. Muslims were more inclined towards farming and other agricultural activities in our area.

The name of our school, Kharkhoda 'Model' School meant that English was taught there. Benches were introduced before partition but only for the English class. When studying English, students used to sit on a bench; at other times they sat on the floor on a *taat*. There was not much difference between this school and others except there were more extra-curricular activities in Aligarh, e.g., dramas, plays, poetry, etc.**"**

Seeing that Lalli had already left, Sardar went to see Binarsi the next morning. There were idols of Hindu gods with garlands and small candles in front of them in every room in Binarsi's house. Sardar was so used to their presence that he had barely noticed them until now. He felt awkward with all these deities staring at him. They seemed to accentuate the difference between his friend's home and his own. He was growing unsure of his welcome. When Binarsi's mother paused for a split second before giving him her customary hug, he wanted to turn around and run back home. Once Binarsi came into the room, Sardar's confusion transcended into excitement at seeing his friend again.

"How's school?" he asked Binarsi later when both boys were sitting near their favourite spot, a hollow in the base of the trunk of a huge banyan tree in the fields near Binarsi's house. They were used to sitting here ever since they were little children. They were too big to sit inside the hollow now, sticking a foot into it sufficed as comfortable nostalgia.

Binarsi sighed. "It's not the same without you and Lalli and my cousin."

Sardar gaped. "Your cousin? Has he left as well?" He knew Binarsi's cousin. They had fought bitterly over a donkey ride when they were six years old; once Sardar had got into trouble for running away with his hat. He sighed bitterly missing the comfort of familiarity.

Binarsi nodded glumly. "Last week. We might leave too."

He shook his head at the stunned look on Sardar's face. "I don't want to go, Sardar. But my parents don't think it's safe here now."

"But why?" Sardar cried aghast. "What's wrong with being here? Who's going to harm you?"

Binarsi looked rather exasperatedly at Sardar. "That's a strange question! Last week my father's friend was pelted with stones…."

"And a couple of months ago, a friend of my uncle's was beaten up by a *Jat* because he was eating beef," Sardar was quick to remind him. "But we're not moving."

"Well, that's because you're in the majority here. There are many more Muslims than Hindus in Kharkhoda. There are just a few Hindu families in this village and the neighbouring one. Being Hindu and in the minority, we might…we might be in danger when people become all excited about who's what and…and such things."

"You forget that almost eighty percent of our teachers in the Model School are Hindu. There are quite a few of the students. There's never been any discrimination between us there."

"The school is not the whole village, Sardar," said Binarsi patiently.

"Who are you in danger from in this village, then? From me? What are you all expecting me to do? Shoot you? Cut off your head? I've had plenty of opportunities, and I haven't done it yet." Sardar said, his face contorted with anger. "Don't you think you're all imagining these things?"

"It's about the entire village." Binarsi threw up his hands in exasperation. "There are other people in this village aside from you, or haven't you noticed? They're not all like you." He sighed. "You don't live at home now, my friend. I do. Maybe that's why you don't know. I hear people talking about these things all the time. It wasn't like that before. Every day they sound a bit more serious, a bit more roused and angry, and…and afraid. It is not just here. It's the same in Delhi. My father and I were there last month. Even if you don't live here anymore and don't know what's going on in Kharkhoda, you must be aware of what's going on in the rest of the country. You must see such things happening in Aligarh."

"No," Sardar said curtly. "In Aligarh there is none of this!"

Binarsi remained adamant. "It is not, okay! But that does not mean it isn't happening. Hindus and Muslims all over India are angry with each other, Sardar. They both want to rid India of the British, but their anger also has to do with…with who will rule when the British are gone."

Sardar stared at his friend. "And who do you think should rule?"

Binarsi shrugged. "I don't know. I only know that I don't want to be killed."

Sardar ran his hand over his face. "So that's why Lalli left. And your cousin. They didn't want me to kill them."

"Hai Ram!" Binarsi made an irritated gesture. "Don't keep saying that! It isn't about you! You're silly!"

"So, I'm silly now," shouted Sardar, jumping to his feet. "You and Lalli have been my oldest friends. Suddenly you think I want to kill you, and that's not crazy!"

Binarsi came to his feet too, and he too was shouting, "Yes, you are my best friend! But you are blind, so blind you don't see what's going on around you! I can't believe Aligarh is as peaceful as you say!"

The two boys glared at each other, breathing heavily. Sardar was the first to recover. He gave an unsteady laugh and clapped Binarsi on the shoulder.

"You need to tell me about my old school. How are the other boys? What're you studying? How's hockey?"

"As usual," Binarsi spoke carefully, trying to sound reasonable. "Oh, we have benches in class now."

"Well, that's a good thing!"

"But we only sit on them when we study English."

Sardar stared at Binarsi, and then both boys burst into whoops of laughter.

"And they want to get rid of the British!" Sardar lay back on the ground, helpless with laughter. "Do they, really?"

"Of course! They'll drive them out riding on benches, shouting 'Out! Get out!' In English!" cried Binarsi, wiping tears from his eyes.

Things appeared to have returned to normal after all that, yet their relationship had changed. It was now based on matters larger than who had the faster bicycle or could throw a ball more accurately at a pile of stones when playing *pithoo*.

Sardar realised Binarsi was right that he, Sardar, was not aware of what was happening around him, nor was he interested in finding out. Politics and its repercussions did not affect him, or so he'd thought. What was happening was why his friends were leaving, why everything appeared to be changing. He was determined to be more perceptive from then on, to try and get his head around the events taking place.

Sardar's mother seemed to understand that there was something profound going on in her eldest son's mind. He could tell she was watching him while the family talked about what was happening in India. He bent his head, pretending to be reading, fixing his hockey stick, oiling his rifle, doing anything to stop from thinking of Binarsi leaving. However, he listened. In the beginning, odd words caught his attention: resolution, protest, majority, angry, scared, discrimination…words he had never paid much attention to before, words he had not cared about. Now they explained what had driven his friends away and made his family so tense.

At the end of July, Sardar and his brothers prepared to return to school. They felt refreshed because being home with their family was always calming, but they were also troubled, because too much had changed, and more change appeared to be in the offing. The changes etched themselves in worry lines on their young faces; there was something almost adult about their appearance.

Sardar and Binarsi had spent as much time together as they could that summer, walking in the orchards, picking and eating fruit, playing cricket, and visiting each place they had known and loved. The did not discuss the present situation of the country or the future again; they allowed themselves to be enveloped by the past memories.

They had said goodbye the day before Sardar left for school. "I'm sorry you're leaving," Sardar had mumbled. "I hope we can meet again someday, when…" Binarsi had simply hugged him then, something neither boy had ever done before. Sardar returned the hug with a fervour that seemed to pull him upwards, like an elastic band he thought wryly.

The next morning, their *yakka* trit-trotted through Kharkhoda on its way to the station. There was the store in front of which the old man used to sit, where he was no longer to be seen. They passed Binarsi's house, the lane to Lalli's house, and then their school. Sardar reminded himself — not that he had forgotten it at any time since he had come to know about it, that the next time he came home Binarsi too would not be there.

The *yakka* left their village and passed through the next one. Remembering the conversations he had heard, Sardar was aware, for the first time of the character of the places he was passing through. He noticed that in Kharkhoda and the next village, there were more mosques than temples. As for Sikh *gurdwaras,* there were none. There were few women with the vermillion dot on their foreheads, or men with the *lungi* draped in a Hindu fashion. But he also noticed that the one butcher shop in the village had been boarded up and someone had scrawled all over the front in chalk. Not knowing the Devanagari script, he did not understand what the scrawls said, but there was a rough scribble in the middle of a knife dripping with blood. He didn't think that was the butcher's logo.

He remembered a conversation between his father and his uncle the night before, "*Bhaijan*, those Hindu *Jats* in the villages surrounding us have become very belligerent all of a sudden," his uncle had said. "That man you sell the wheat to, he looked at me in a very hostile way when I took mine to him the other day. He set ridiculous terms of sale, but he refused to budge. There was a message there for sure." Sardar's father had looked worried. "They control access to our village. Please don't anger them if you can help it."

The *yakka* arrived at the train station.

4th October, 2016

Syed Sardar Ahmad:

"It took me just six months to learn English and cope with speaking it because I was in an environment where I heard English everywhere.

It made no difference at school, whether someone came from a poor or rich background. A person's social class was never on our minds there. The son of the man who used to clean my room was my

73

class fellow, and both of us wore black *sherwanis*, so there was no difference, and I never thought of him as a son of a cleaner. Let me tell you that though we have Pakistan now, Allah *ka shukar* for that, we have lost our heritage. There are no institutions, and there are no traditions; how will we ever get back our tradition is something that worries me.**"**

"I must be imagining it of course," said Sardar when he and his brothers passed the large portrait of Sir Syed Ahmad Khan in the main foyer, the day after arriving at Aligarh, "but he is not frowning at me as I thought he was before." Mukhtar and Salar stared at the portrait too, and they agreed. Sir Syed's eyes seemed benign now; the bushy white beard fanning out peacefully on his chest, no longer appeared to bristle as it had when they had seen the portrait as new students.

"It's called being at home in a place," someone said behind them. They turned to find one of their teachers there. "Welcome back, boys," he said with a smile.

Returning to school after a holiday at home was definitely a different experience than coming to school for the first time. The surroundings were not new anymore and they felt at home now, as their teacher had pointed out, and that they had learnt a lot since they started here. The boys greeted friends and exchanged holiday stories.

"Stop it," said Sardar one day when Mukhtar stuck out his tongue at him.

Mukhtar stuck out his tongue again.

"Fine then," said Sardar. "Keep doing it." He spoke in Urdu, before adding in English, "You are behaving like an impudent child." He walked away, leaving Mukhtar standing stock-still, wondering what to respond with.

Yes, one of the things he had learnt was English. Sardar couldn't resist writing to his mother about the incident. She wrote back, amused.

But notice this, she wrote. You and Mukhtar are very different. You fight and call each other names. But you still care about each other as brothers should. There are other people who are very different from you. You still have to respect them. Have you thought about this?

Sardar had not thought about it, but he did now. What makes people respect each other, he thought wonderingly?

It isn't sharing the same language.

They heard several languages in school because Aligarh had students from Bihar, Gujrat, Baluchistan, Sindh, and Pashtuns from the Frontier. One of Sardar's good friends in school was from Sylhet in Bengal, and another from Lahore, in Punjab. He had learnt to enquire 'how are you' to one by saying "Kemon achen?" and to the other 'Wal changay o? Most students could speak Urdu, and almost all were able to speak English, while some were good at it.

A friend of Sardar's from Lahore was Shia, but Sardar was aware of this only because they said their prayers at different times at the mosque. Considering his other even closer friends in Kharkhoda were Hindu, religion is not what determined respect and friendship either. Nor is it the colour of the skin, he added to himself, recalling the dearth of respect the *goras* were facing in India.

If it's none of these things, he wondered, how about financial status? He gave a sidelong glance at one of his classmates who was dressed like Sardar himself in a black *sherwani*, and who sat playing chess with some other boys. Sardar's father was a rich landlord, and this classmate's father a boot-repairer for the *sarkar*.

"Yet we are very alike," Sardar thought, suddenly grateful that he had never thought of the boy as being any different. "Except that he is better at history than I am," he remembered recent assignment ruefully.

Perhaps it was the values they were taught — they must be responsible for their non-discriminatory friendships. When Aligarh students went to the city to see a movie or have a bite to eat, people seemed to hold them in high regard.

"Ah, from Aligarh," said the man at the ticket window, when Sardar and his friends went to see 'Boys Will be Boys,' Sardar's first English movie, a comedy set around the disappearance of a valuable necklace in a school. "We have some excellent seats for you."

"Won't they be expensive?" one boy asked.

The man smiled. "We give our best seats at concessional rates to students from your school," he said. They realised he was right when they paid what they would for standard gallery seats but were seated where they had the best view of the screen.

Across the aisle from them was an English couple, the blonde young man holding the girl's hand. This public display of affection, so unusual in India, seemed to make the boys from Aligarh uncomfortable. When Sardar looked at his friends, he realised that each of them had twisted a little in his seat. It made him smile. Yes, differences existed, yet no one was threatening the young couple.

The Second World War started in 1939. In January 1940, Britain called in 2,000,000 of its young men between the ages of 19 to 27 to join its army. The Indian army, too, had been brought into the war. In May, Neville Chamberlain was replaced as Prime Minister by Winston Churchill.

When the boys went to see 'Boys Will be Boys', the film started

— as all movies did now with Churchill's rallying speech in Parliament:

"…we shall not flag or fail," said Churchill. "We shall go on to the end; we shall fight in France; we shall fight on the seas and oceans; we shall fight with growing confidence and growing strength in the air; we shall defend our Island, whatever the cost may be, we shall fight on the beaches, we shall fight on the landing grounds, we shall fight in the fields and in the streets, we shall fight in the hills; we shall never surrender…"

Many students of Aligarh had relatives in the war, making up the thousands and later millions of Indians fighting in the Second World War. Their thoughts were naturally never far from the battlefields, but that speech brought the war even more into the immediate sphere for them.

Mukhtar had seen the film too; his thoughts were more on Churchill's speech than on the movie. "Well, suddenly, 'we' means us all — the British and the Indians!" he mocked. "How convenient! Churchill is sending us Indians to fight so we can be killed and injured in a war that belongs to him and his countrymen. I find that outrageous, don't you?" he glared around at the other boys when they returned to school as if challenging them to contradict him. They did not.

Sardar was there too. He realised that for Mukhtar politics struck more chords than for him. But he said nothing. In his pocket was a letter from their mother. Riffat Bano generally wrote to all three sons together. He indicated they should follow him to one side of the room so he could read it out.

Your father's friend is home from the war, she wrote. He has lost half his arm. Pray for him. He is in pain. We insisted he, along with his family, come stay with us. We will look after him, all of us together. They send their love to the three of you.

Sardar laid down the letter and smoothed it out with his hand. "I heard one of the teachers say more than 200,000 Indians have joined the army."

"My God!" said Mukhtar pushing his head back. "That's even worse than I thought."

Otherwise, while the war raged in the outer world, life in Aligarh continued at its usual steady pace. Once you put on the *sherwani* and cap, tucked the handkerchief into your pocket and walked into the classroom, life outside seemed to recede into the background.

Time passed. One of their teachers wrote a poem about it:

> The present crumbles into the river of time,
>
> And returns as the future on the other side,
>
> Distant, unreachable, unknown,
>
> Now is where we are born, and then we die,
>
> Slick with the silt of time.

6th October, 2016

Syed Sardar Ahmad:

"Mukhtar was a bit different, so after two years at Aligarh he was transferred to *Jamia* where there was more discipline; everything had to be done on your own like making your bed, cleaning your room. Salar and I remained in Aligarh.

I only paid attention to what was said about the Muslim League and Jinnah in 1942. Quaid-e-Azam, Nishtar Sahib, Liaquat Ali Khan, Raja Ghazanfar, Raja Sahib of Mehmoodabad and others used to come to Aligarh. I saw Jinnah for the first time in 1943 or 1944. I am telling you that hardly any of us understood Jinnah's English, but we knew that whatever he was saying was worth paying attention to. There was pin-drop silence while he spoke. Students would clap wherever appropriate; he was greeted with adoration, listened to attentively, and people would ask him questions with great respect. The students of our university loved him.

Whenever he was in Aligarh, he would always be wearing a *sherwani* and never a suit, along with a *chouridar* pyjama and his Jinnah cap."

In 1942, the Second World War was in its third year, the brothers were in Kharkhoda for their holidays before the start of the new school year — as they were every year. On their second day at home, Sardar looked up from the book he was reading to see Mukhtar looking dazed.

"What's the matter?" said Sardar, as Mukhtar fell on his own bed, dropped his head back on his linked hands and lay staring into space. When Mukhtar did not reply, Sardar put his book down and got up, "Mukhtar?"

"I'm leaving Aligarh," Mukhtar said without looking at his brother.

"*What?*"

"I'm leaving Aligarh," repeated Mukhtar. He jumped up and waved his hand in Sardar's face. "I'm leaving, brother mine!," Sardar realised with bewildered astonishment that Mukhtar was not upset at all, as he, Sardar would have been if he were leaving Aligarh because Sardar had grown to love his new school. Instead, Mukhtar's face was positively glowing.

"You're leaving school?" Sardar couldn't believe his parents would let any of them do that.

"Tsk! Of course not! I'm leaving Aligarh, not school! I'm changing schools. I'm moving to *Jamia*! *Jamia Millia Islamia*!"

Sardar had only ever seen that look in his brother's eyes when he was reading Iqbal or Jauhar's poetry.

Failing to get anything rational from Mukhtar, Sardar strode off to his parents' room and sat beside his mother while she finished her *namaz* and a long *dua* for each member of the family. Then they talked.

"He doesn't fit in the way Salar and you do, *beta*," his mother explained. "I understood what it was when I saw the books he was reading. Still, I decided to give him some time to settle in, but he didn't. He will at *Jamia*; it will be more to his liking *In Sha Allah*. He's interested in politics and religion. There he will get both, a greater sense of participation in current affairs and a better grounding in religion. Besides, you know, one of the founding fathers of the school, Muhammad Ali Jauhar, is a hero to your brother."

Sardar gave a half-smile. "Yes. Well, moving might be a good idea then, *Apajan*. Where is *Jamia*? Is it in Aligarh too? No, it isn't. I seem to remember someone saying…"

"It used to be in Aligarh," Riffat Bano nodded, "but it moved a few years ago to a small village near Delhi called Okhla. We'll visit it when Mukhtar's there. They're more strict with their discipline at *Jamia*, and the students are expected to look after themselves much more than at Aligarh. Housekeeping does not do everything. He'll make his own bed, and the boys will take turns to do the cleaning. It will be good for Mukhtar."

Apajan understood Mukhtar better than anyone else, but even so, Sardar was not sure his mother was right. "He can't even manage his socks and handkerchiefs, *Apajan*," Sardar laughed. "How will he do all that?"

"He will because he will be on his own. He finds it confusing when there are too many people involved with what he does. Most importantly, the responsibility will be his alone. He'll sort himself out, you wait and see."

When Sardar, Mukhtar and Salar went back to school that year, Mukhtar stayed back in Delhi. He would make his way separately to Okhla from there. The other two carried on, taking the next train to Aligarh.

Mukhtar's letters from his new school were full of news, most of it political. In August that year, Mukhtar wrote about the Quit India Movement and all the leaders who had been arrested. "Gandhi said *'Mere jail jaane se kuch nahi hoga; karo ya maro* (do or die)' And he is now in prison."

He wrote about the famine in Bengal, condemning the government for creating conditions that led to the famine, and never formally recognising the emergency. Sardar spoke to his Bengali friends in school after that letter and got more details. He was horrified to know that millions, not thousands had died in the famine and many more were likely to.

It was mostly because of Mukhtar's letters that Sardar started taking an interest in these events, consequently in the Muslim League and Jinnah; it was then he understood the cause they represented.

Jinnah, Abdur Rab Nishtar, Liaquat Ali Khan, Raja Ghazanfar, Raja Sahib of Mehmoodabad, and others, they all visited Aligarh University at some time or the other. Although Jinnah had visited the University before, it was not until the 10th of March 1944 that Sardar saw him for the first time. Jinnah came to address the student's union, a tall, thin figure in a *sherwani* and *chouridaar pyjama* walking up the path towards the venue of the meeting. On his head was the woollen cap that had come to be associated with the man himself and which was now called a 'Jinnah cap.' He was surrounded by a group of students, all listening intently to what he was saying.

"There was no need for him to raise his voice when he spoke to us," Sardar's friend's brother who was in the union told a group of students later in the common room. "We all listened in utter silence to everything he had to say, and whenever he stopped speaking, we clapped, and we clapped! He has such a following and such a formidable presence!"

"What did he say to you?" one of the boys asked.

"He said, 'Five years ago did anybody talk about us, or did anybody care to know who we were, and what we wanted?'"

I didn't even know until very recently, thought Sardar guiltily.

"'But a great change has come about during the last few years,' he said. 'There is not a day when every newspaper, friendly or unfriendly, does not talk about the Muslim League....we stand by our conviction, and neither flattery nor coercion can divert us from our determined purpose.'"

"You should have seen the way everyone clapped then!" the friend's brother said, an awed look on his face.

Sardar's English was still not good enough to allow him to understand everything Jinnah said. However, he understood and agreed with Jinnah's response to a student who asked what sort of government they would have if they ever carved out another country from India.

"Pakistan came into being when the very first Hindu converted into Muslim, it happened, when there was no rule of Muslims. The foundation of Muslims is *Kalma-e-Tauheed* rather than state or race. When a Hindu converted his religion, he became a member of a separate nation and a new nation came into being."

Later that year, in the middle of the night, a large number of students stood on one of the platforms at the railway station, Sardar among them. They were there because they had heard that

Jinnah's train was to pass through the station, and they wanted another glimpse of the man they had learnt to admire so much.

"It's here," the young man next to Sardar said excitedly. "It's here!" All heads swivelled towards the dark tunnel from which trains issued onto the platform. Two sharp lights pierced the darkness and grew steadily larger. The noise of the approaching train filled the station, and the platform on which they stood shook. The students put their arms up to wave the train to a stop. One foolhardy young man seemed ready to jump onto the tracks, ostensibly to block its path.

"I want to see Jinnah!" he cried when his friends grabbed hold of him.

"So you will, you imbecile, in your next life, if you get any closer to the edge!" his rescuers said firmly.

The train driver probably realised it was dangerous to forge through such a swarm of enthusiasm because the train puffed and whistled to a stop. The clamour became even louder then.

The students waved and shouted: "Jinnah sahib *zindabad*! Long live Jinnah!" and "Jinnah *hamara leader hai*!" Jinnah is our leader!

Knowing they were far from their destination yet, the blinds in every compartment were down, and the occupants slept. But when the train stopped amidst such deafening noise, blinds and gauze curtains twitched, and some passengers looked out cautiously, worried they were caught in one of the violent riots that were taking place all over the country.

"What's going on?" Jinnah inquired of his secretary, who had the bunk opposite his in a compartment somewhere in the middle of the train. The secretary apprised him of the situation and advised him not to leave the train for the sake of his own security. But Jinnah was a man with a purpose and not one for letting such opportunities slip away. He donned his *sherwani*, and set his cap.

"We want Jinnah! We want Jinnah!" the students shouted.

The blinds and then the window belonging to Jinnah's compartment went up, and a cheer arose on the platform, followed by a deafening roar when Jinnah stuck his head out to greet the students.

Jinnah raised his hand, and there was instant silence on the platform.

"I have put questions to all sorts of our people, *Mussalmans*, on the countryside, and at different gatherings, at railway stations, I have asked them what do you mean by Pakistan, and I tell you that I was astonished at the *Kisans* and railway workers when they give me their answers...I asked at one of the railway stations, at a gathering of nearly 500 people, what do you understand by Pakistan? The answer came from among those people; one man said, 'By Pakistan, I understand that I do not want Central Government for the whole of India, it means Hindu Raj and the provinces where we are in a majority will be under the yoke of Hindus.' When I said that what do you then want? He said, 'I want first where the Muslims are in the majority, we should have our independent government nothing to do with the Centre of Hindu India'...Then I asked him because he was in the C.P. where Muslims are only 4 percent, what will happen to you who are here 4 percent. He said, 'It is my misfortune that I am born here; let my brethren have their own *Hukumat* and let them at least be free. God will protect us here.' We do not wish ill to the Hindus..."

Raising his hand in farewell, he drew back into the compartment and lowered the blind once again. The train left amidst cheers as the students moved back, filled with excitement at having seen and heard their leader.

They were walking back to school when a car came down the road. It was making a strange flapping sound, and it stopped a little after the crossing. Two men got off, one an Indian in uniform and cap, obviously the driver, and an Englishman wearing trousers and a slightly crumpled shirt. The latter stood by the roadside while the first opened the trunk of the car. There were women in the back seat; one of them opened her door. Seeing the large group of boys, she closed it again, and the man moved deliberately between the car and the boys as if to veil its occupants. Behind him, the driver left the trunk and moved to stand beside his employer as well.

One of the boys in front of the group laughed. "Force of numbers, see my friends? Even the *angraiz sarkar* is afraid of us when we're all together."

The Englishman moved forward threateningly, gripping his walking stick.

"Don't worry *farangi* sahib," said the same boy. "We've been to see someone much greater than you can possibly be, and he wouldn't approve if we got into a tiff with you like this." He gave a disdainful smile and was about to lead the boys to the other side of the road when his eye fell upon the car's flat tire.

"Don't you have a spare?" he said roughly.

"We have," the Englishman said in clipped tones. "Kindly carry on with your walk."

The boy, however, stood his ground and speaking to the driver in Urdu repeated his question. The man gave a nervous look at his employer and said in a mixture of English and Urdu, "Stepney also no hawa." The spare tire has no air.

The boy turned to the other students. "If we leave them here, someone might hurt them. It isn't safe these days. What do you say?"

Sardar and the other boys were ready to help. Together, they took turns to push the car to a service station about ten miles away. They helped the driver pump up the spare tire and fit it to the car. The Englishman tried to thank them, but the boys didn't stop to listen. When the car had left, the boy who had taken the lead doubled up laughing.

"What's wrong with you?" Sardar gave him a questioning look.

"I had this rubber toy in my pocket, it belonged to my little brother, and he gave it to me when I came here. He said it would remind me of home and him."

"So…what about it?"

"Well let's put it this way. I hope the Englishman is not scared of mice because he's sitting on one now, even if it's just rubber. It will squeak when he moves."

7th October, 2016

Syed Sardar Ahmad:

"I did my matriculation from Aligarh College and then enrolled in F.Com, to study commerce. I didn't complete it. I was in my second year of F.Com. when Partition took place. In 1947 everything came to a sudden halt for most of us.

Before that, elections were held in 1946. The Muslim league contested from all over India. Iqbal's vision, in the light of the Pakistan movement, was explained to the public and propagated all over the country.

We, the students, were split into small groups of around five or six; each group travelled to different villages to solicit votes for the Muslim League. I remember my group. It consisted of a few other students and me, and included Zawwar Hussain Zaidi, later Dr Zawwar Hussain Zaidi. He is a prominent figure of the Pakistan Movement. He studied at Aligarh Muslim University and did his M.A and LLB there. He was the author of twenty books. Thirteen of these are in English, six in Urdu, and one in Persian. Later on, he was appointed as the head of the history department in FC College, Lahore. He also taught at the Punjab University and School of Oriental and African Studies (SOAS), London, for 42 years. He worked for UNESCO's International Council of Archives for ten years.

In 1982, he came to Pakistan from London in order to compile the Muslim League Papers and the Quaid-e-Azam Papers, which were lying in the National Archives department. He loved Jinnah and was very inspired by him. He would say, *'Delhi walon se pocho shaan hamari'* — ask the people of Delhi how wonderful we are.

We were given trucks on which we travelled to different villages to ask for votes. We used to try to make people understand that the survival and benefit of the Muslims of India depended on this dream the Muslim League has perceived for us. "The British will soon be leaving," we said. "If you don't vote for the League, you'll be left with Hindus ruling over you, and you will be their slaves".

We were going to a village one night when we were stopped by some Muslim men. They said, "This village has more Hindus than Muslims. Every Muslim vote here is yours, but don't go any further, or they will beat you up and humiliate you." We were then directed to a dairy farm for the night. I don't remember its name, but it was a village in UP, and we had travelled about 50 miles from Aligarh. We spent the night hidden away in hay and cow dung.

In other places, we actually *were* beaten up.

The Hindus were united in their hate for the Muslim League, while the Muslims were divided in how they felt about it. This was their home; they did not call it a sub-continent but called it their country. They could not imagine dividing their home into two parts, and then there were those who supported the idea of a separate homeland. The love and goodwill for the Muslim League were quite clear. The students of Islamia College and the Aligarh University worked hard and played their part in making the dream of Pakistan possible.**"**

In December 1945, the Indian general elections took place, and provincial elections were scheduled for the following month in January 1946. Sardar was about to start his first year of college to study commerce.

Mukhtar appeared to have settled into *Jamia*. He was always reminding his brothers to do more.

"We need to be as active as possible in these elections," he wrote to them. "Tell your friends be a united front in supporting our leaders."

Indeed, it was no longer possible to be indifferent to the politics of the day. It touched too many of them personally. The boy who shared a desk with Sardar was one of many who lost relatives in the war; he had lost his eldest brother.

When Sardar expressed his sympathy, the boy said, "My brother was so energetic, so full of life," his voice almost harsh, he was trying so hard not to break down. "I simply cannot imagine him just lying there…" He stopped abruptly, to collect himself.

After a while, he spoke again. "I'm going home in a few days when he comes…when he is brought home." He shivered. "I suppose we're fortunate. There are so many who have not come back at all, and their families will never know if they are alive or dead."

"Yes," Sardar sighed. "You heard what our teacher said today about Japanese POW camps, being dead is better than being in one of them. There are so many being tortured in those camps. We must be grateful as you say when someone loses his life without…" He put his arm around his friend's shoulder, and they sat there for a while in silence.

The sentiment against Japan was tempered by pity and horror on the 6th of August that year when the United States detonated its first atomic bomb over the Japanese city of Hiroshima, destroying more than half the city and killing thousands of people. A hush lay over the school when the news broke that evening.

"I can't even…can't even begin to imagine so many people dying!" one of the boys said during the English class the next day.

Another boy, whose family lived in Sylhet, pointed out the fatalities in Hiroshima were still not as bad as the ones in the famine in Bengal a couple of years ago.

"Millions died in that famine," he said bitterly. "Millions. What is a 100,000 or so by comparison?"

Their teacher, a young man, was listening quietly to this conversation. When the boys had said what they had to, he picked up his chalk and drew a circle on the board. "That's one person dead," he said, and he had everyone's attention.

He drew five more circles and connected them with lines to the dead person. "That's five children. Oh and…" he drew another ten circles and connecting them to the first as well. "That is the dead man's wife, his parents and his brothers and sisters. I'm presuming he has no grandparents living and no friends. That would add many more circles, but there is not enough space on this board."

Not a single student spoke.

"Every death," the teacher said softly, "is a tragedy for at least fifteen people, more often more. Each of you knows how much it would hurt to lose a parent or a brother or sister, or even a friend you love. So," the teacher looked around at his students who one and all had stricken expressions on their faces. "So, what does it matter if one person dies or ten? Every single death is a tragedy; every single murder a crime. Do you know what our Prophet Muhammad (Peace be upon him) said about murder?"

"He forbade it," ventured one of the boys.

"Yes, of course, he did," said the teacher. "Killing is such a big crime that our Prophet Muhammad, may peace be upon him, said that 'the first cases to be decided on the Day of Judgement will be those of bloodshed.' But," he added. "It is a sad fact that on this earth, murder is not always punished. Have you boys heard about Voltaire?"

None of them had, so the teacher wrote the name in the corner of the board beside his diagram. "He was French, and a famous writer, who also wrote in English. One of his most remarkable books is a novel called Candide. It was Voltaire who said that 'It is forbidden to kill; therefore, all murderers are punished unless they kill in large numbers, and to the sound of trumpets.' What do you suppose he meant?"

He gave the boys time to think; it was Sardar who answered him first.

"Did he mean that it was not easy to punish someone who kills hundreds of people?" he said tentatively.

The teacher nodded. "That's good. Yes. He was saying that when you kill one man or two, you go to prison and are punished... most of the time. But when large armies and strong countries kill hundreds or thousands of people, they are not punished. Why? I want you to think about this in light of what has happened in Japan."

It was a thoughtful bunch of boys that filed out of the class that day, and they were still discussing the matter when three days later another atomic bomb fell, this time on the city of Nagasaki, killing thousands of people again.

So, Sardar knew what he meant when on the 2nd of September 1945, the man who cleaned their dormitory sat in a corner muttering "*Allah ka shukr*! Thank God! Thank God!" to himself, his head in his hands. It was because the Japanese had surrendered that day.

The surrender meant an end to the Second World War, and to the senseless massacre all over the world. India breathed an enormous sigh of relief, along with the Allied powers. For Indians, their greatest hope was that perhaps now the survivors amongst the 2.5 million Indian soldiers who had fought in the war — it was said that 87,000 of them had died — would finally come home...

Now Jinnah, Iqbal, Wavell, Bose, Gandhi were part of every conversation. Calls for the British to honour their promise and leave India had become strident. The urgency for creation of Pakistan reflected in every discussion. Every evening, in the common rooms, the students crowded around the radio to listen to A.S Bokhari's Hindi news commentary on All India Radio or one of the many programmes in other Indian languages.

"Only the Muslims of this country themselves can help each other escape the pit into which they are in danger of falling," one of their teachers said. "The public has no concept of what, most likely, awaits us in the future. We need to explain it to people personally, to remind them of the Lahore Resolution. Not many of our people can read. Very few possess radios."

A few days before the elections, the same teacher stood before the class.

"I need volunteers," he said. "Students who will travel the countryside and canvas for the Muslim League and Mohammad Ali Jinnah.

"Me! I'll do it!" Sardar said eagerly, and he was one of several other boys to be recruited for the task. They were organised into groups and provided with transport and drivers. The boys introduced themselves to each other. Zawwar Hussain Zaidi, in Sardar's group, was known at Aligarh as one of the most fervent supporters of Jinnah.

Over the next few days, their group visited several villages in their beaten-down old truck. Some people in those villages were welcoming, others hostile. The boys could never be sure which way things would turn out.

The first day they visited a nearby village with a predominance of Muslims.

"Come and share our *roti* with us," the headman invited them.

The boys accepted gladly and followed him to a small village surrounded by a fringe of trees. The houses were modest, made of rough brick with thatched roofs. In the centre was a dusty open space dotted with cattle, piles of wood, the inevitable hand pump, barrels of water and sundry other things. Here, the village men and the boys from Aligarh sat on charpoys near a house with a bright blue door, sipping hot, sweet, milky tea. The women watched from a distance, their children gawking open-mouthed at the boys.

After a short discussion about the elections and how to vote, the students addressed the headman and solicited the support of his people for the Muslim League. "Jinnah depends on you," they said. "The Muslims of this country need your vote."

"Sure, the League has our votes," said the village headman, an old man whose white turban contrasted magnificently with his chocolate brown skin. "Every Muslim in this village is very clear about his allegiance."

Then a young man stood up and said "For centuries Muslims and Hindus have lived together. We ruled over them once, yes, many years ago, but they are also our friends. Our next-door neighbour is Hindu, yesterday my wife was ill, so his wife made *chapatti* for us and helped look after our children. I'm just a poor village man, but I know that the Muslim League wants to give Muslims and Hindus separate homelands. Is that the only way to solve our problems?"

"The Muslim League wants a separate homeland for the Muslims of India," said Sardar. "But that does not mean it wants us to make enemies of our Hindu friends. It only means that we must think of the future and the dangers of a time where differences may override harmony."

"Yes," agreed another boy. "Times change, and with them our requirements. The people a man was once closest to can become his most dangerous enemies."

The young villager looked uncertain but said nothing more.

"You must realise that when the British leave, we will be left facing the Hindus who are in the majority," Sardar said. "There is likely to be a bloody tussle for the upper hand. They will not want us to rule them again. There is a good chance we will end up being their slaves this time. I don't think any of us want that. The Partition of India is inevitable, so now is the best time to make sure we get our demands." He looked around at the men in front of him. "Do you remember what Iqbal said? He said, *'It is true that we are made of dust, and the world is made of dust. But that dust contains dust motes, and they (dust motes) are rising.'*"

Later, the boys ventured further than this first village. Almost fifty miles from Aligarh, they found themselves looking for a place to settle down for the night. When they saw a group of four villagers, they stopped for directions to make sure they were on the right track. The men asked them why they were there.

"We're here to speak to the people about the elections," said Sardar.

The men eyed the boys closely. "You're from the Muslim League?" one of them said abruptly.

Praying that they were not hostile to the League, Sardar accepted that they were from the League.

"Well, you don't need to fear us," the man replied, gesturing towards his companions. "We'll vote for the Muslim League, but our village there," he nodded down the road, "it contains a majority of Hindus. I suggest you do not go there. Not everyone will welcome you, and some of the villagers might even get violent."

The boys had hoped to rest for the night. Understanding their worried looks, the men directed them back down the lane.

"You'll find a shed belonging to a dairy farm at the end of the lane on the right. You can stay the night there," they said, "but make sure you leave very early in the morning before the farm workers arrive."

Following their instructions, the boys went back down the road they had travelled a few minutes ago. There were fields on either side, with knee-high alfalfa and grass. The fields were deserted.

"If it had been earlier in the day, we would have looked for another town or village nearby," one of the boys said with a sigh.

"They might not have welcomed us either," Sardar pointed out.

"True," said the other boy with a rueful grin.

They turned right as instructed onto an even more rutted lane, which led to a large, brick barn.

"Well, it looks like we are spending the night here," said Sardar as clearly as he could for the bumps.

The driver stopped the truck. They all stepped out and eyed the barn doubtfully.

"Moooo!" came a sleepy greeting from behind the walls. The boys opened the door and walked in. It was a large space, dimly lit with dusty glass windows set high up into the walls. Pillars held up the roof, and each pillar was surrounded by a food trough. There were more troughs at either end containing water, which was responsible for the mosquitoes filling the barn.

"You have a choice between letting yourself being bitten by a buffalo or a mosquito," said one of the boys gloomily. "Cover yourselves as best as you can."

"It's a good thing we brought something to eat," said another, handing out *parathas* and water. "Shoo!" as a buffalo came wandering too close. The animal blinked its large black eyes at the human in front of it and ducked its head a couple of times. The huge grey horns on its head curled menacingly towards them, and the boys drew back instinctively. One of them, a son of a dairy farm owner laughed and patted the buffalo.

"Relax," he said. "They look aggressive, but they aren't. Why are *you* scared of them?" he asked Sardar. "I thought you lived on a farm as well."

"I do, but not on a dairy farm," shrugged Sardar. "I'm not scared of them. I just don't like them…," he held up his palm in front of his face, "…so close to me."

Sardar, his friends and the truck driver spent that night on beds of straw and hay surrounded by the drowsy herd. They hadn't expected to sleep, but they did and were woken up by Zawwar's yells as one of the great black animals breathed a gusty sigh of warm air all over him. Roused early morning by this chaos, they got ready to leave before any hustle bustle ensued.

They left just before sunrise, damp, dirty, itchy and sleepy.

"I presume this lot does not support the Muslim League," Sardar cried then, running with the other boys, all of them with their arms over their heads to escape the stones sailing over them. They were being chased to their truck by the passers-by in saffron dhotis who were probably the residents of a nearby village that they were warned about last night.

At yet another settlement, also with a mixed Hindu Muslim population, they were asked with considerable hostility, "What's so wonderful about you that you come here telling us what to do and whom to vote for?"

"*Dilli wallon say poocho shaan hamari*," quoted Zaidi. "Ask the people of Delhi to tell you how wonderful we are!"

The villagers hooted. "*Abbay, Dilli wallay tum say poochain kis nay tori taang tumhari! Hoy*! The people of Delhi should ask you who it was that broke your legs." They ran angrily towards the boys brandishing sticks and shouting. As they ran for their lives, Sardar noticed some villagers peeping from their huts. Were these the scared Muslims, he wondered later, who, being in the minority, did not feel safe joining the discussion?

With an extra spurt of speed, they made it to their truck. Mercifully for them, the driver had not switched off the engine or they would have lost their head-start in the time it took to crank it up again.

"Power to the Lahore Resolution!" shouted Sardar out of the window as their truck began moving, another boy added, "*Bun kay rahay ga Pakistan!*"

The men were enveloped in smoke and dust as the truck moved off in a hail of stones.

When the election results were announced, it turned out that the Indian Congress had won more than half the seats.

"After all that, the Muslim League lost," said Sardar gloomily, when he and some of his friends were discussing the elections with their economics teacher.

"Yes, it did," said the teacher, "but don't lose heart, the League won all the Muslim votes."

"So?" Sardar said. "How does that help?"

"Well, Sardar, the Muslims are in the minority in India so quite expectedly, they lost. They were never going to convince the Hindus to support their vision. But remember, Muslims are a large minority, big enough to possess clout. These results mean that the League managed to unite the Muslims. That is very important. Nothing can be achieved without that. Most importantly it means that all negotiations with the Muslims will now have to go through the League," he threw up his hands "which is now the only party that represents the Muslims of India. And we all know what the League wants."

"Pakistan!" said the boys, sitting up again, looking suddenly more cheerful.

"Yes," smiled the teacher.

8th October, 2016

Syed Sardar Ahmad:

"In March 1947, Tara Singh drew out his sword in front of the assembly hall and said challengingly, 'I will see how Pakistan is made.' During the Partition of India, over one million Sikhs, Hindus and Muslims were killed, and around ten to twenty million families were displaced as they migrated across the new India-Pakistan border. During this period, many alleged that Tara Singh endorsed the ruthless killing. On 3 March 1947, at Lahore, Singh along with about

500 Sikhs declared from a dais "Death to Pakistan." We are witness to this. On the 3rd of June 1947, an announcement was made on the radio, which said that the Partition of India would take place in August 1947.

The Muslims were very happy, but the Hindus were not happy at all. This observation can be drawn by the later murder of Mahatma Gandhi, who was such a popular Hindu leader. He was killed by Godse, one reason for this murder was that Gandhi said Pakistan's government should receive its rightful share of resources. Gandhi had only agreed to give us the rightful share, and that in itself was unacceptable by the fundamental mindset. You can assess the level of bias against Pakistan from this.

I was in Kharkhoda in August 1947. The violence did not start until after the 14th of August. It started early in Bihar, where numerous violent incidents took place but there was no violence in other parts of India until Partition actually took place. This is mere observation based on my knowledge and what I saw.

The violence happened because of the weakness of our leaders, both Muslims and Hindu. They were perhaps unable to foresee how things would unfold after Partition. They should not have accepted the date of independence unless all our assets, all our police, all our army were transferred from India to Pakistan. This was the weakness of our movement that they were unable to gauge how matters would escalate. Things happened so fast, so extremely fast after 14th August, in a way that was impossible to foresee.**"**

The summer holidays started in the middle of May. Mukhtar came back to Kharkhoda a couple of days before Sardar and Salar. All three found home to be a very different place to the one they had left behind earlier that year. Everyone was stressed and uncertain because trouble was in the offing. The tension was like a hissing, tongue-flicking snake within each person, coiled and ready to spring. Their uncles came more often to their parents' house to discuss what was happening. The family was not always on the same side in these discussions.

On the 3rd of June 1947, all of them, Sardar's grandparents, parents, uncles, siblings and cousins, were at Meer Meherbaan Ali's house, Sardar's ancestral home. They were huddled around a large polished wooden radio set with a gold brocade front. They were waiting for a speech by the Viceroy of India.

"Prince Louis Francis Albert Victor Nicholas of Battenberg, the first Earl Mountbatten of Burma."

"What…?" said Mukhtar, he was hushed as the announcement they were waiting for came on the air.

"You will now hear a statement from Prime Minister Attlee, followed by a message from Lord Mountbatten, the Viceroy of India," it said.

"I would make an earnest appeal to everyone to give calm and dispassionate consideration to these proposals," the Prime Minister went on. "It is, of course, easy to criticise them, but weeks of devoted work by the Viceroy have failed to find an alternative that is practicable. They have emerged from the hard facts of the situation in India".

A…a…choo!" sneezed one of Sardar's cousins. Several hands went up to shush the unfortunate little girl as Lord Mountbatten came on air. There was silence in the room to hear him speak on behalf of the British Monarch.

"A statement will be read to you tonight, giving the final decision of his Majesty's Government as to the method by which power will be transferred from British to Indian hands. But before this happens, I want to give a personal message to the people of India, as well as a short account of the discussions which I have held with the leaders of the political parties, and which have led up to the advice I tendered to His Majesty's Government during my recent visit to London."

Halfway through his speech, Lord Mountbatten said, "The way is now open for an arrangement in which power can be transferred many months earlier than the most optimistic of us thought possible…"

At those words, the people in the room thrust their fists into the air in silent jubilation before listening to what else Mountbatten had to say. "…and, at the same time, leave it to the people of British India to decide for themselves on their future, which is the declared policy of his Majesty's Government."

When the end of the speech came with the words 'I have faith in the future of India and am proud to be with you all at this momentous time. May your decisions be wisely guided, and may they be carried out in the peaceful and friendly spirit of the Gandhi-Jinnah appeal,' the room erupted in cheers, and fervent 'Amens'. The details did not matter yet. The fact that the people of India were soon to be rid of colonial rule was sufficient for now.

"What does he mean we can decide for ourselves?" Salar asked.

"He means when India is independent, In Sha Allah, its people will be free to choose whether we wish to stay together or split into two separate countries," Sharif Ahmad replied. "Let's hope it will be a peaceful process. Listen to what Nehru has to say now."

Everyone quietened down again, and when Jinnah spoke after

Nehru, they huddled even closer to the radio.

Jinnah said: "Grave responsibility lies particularly on the shoulders of Indian leaders. Therefore, we must galvanise and concentrate all our energy to see that the transfer of power is affected in a peaceful and orderly manner. I most earnestly appeal to every community and particularly to Muslim India to maintain peace and order. We must examine the plan, in its letter and in its spirit and come to our conclusions and make our decisions. I pray to God that at this critical moment, He may guide us and enable us to discharge our responsibilities in a wise and statesmanlike manner. Once more I most earnestly appeal to all to maintain peace and order."

Jinnah ended by saying: "Pakistan Zindabad."

There were cheers and applause around the room as the broadcast ended with Baldev Singh's speech.

"We need to remember what Jinnah said before," Sardar's youngest uncle said. "Remember, 'At present, you should believe in Pakistan and then take the idea forward one step at a time.'"

"Well, this is step one," said Mukhtar.

"A huge one," Sardar reminded him fervently.

"The British could not have stayed on," another uncle said. "They spent too much on the war. We are proving a heavy burden on their economy for now."

"Well, they certainly tried to lighten the load," said Sardar's father dryly. "India is lighter by...how many, more than 80,000 Indians? The result of a war that was not ours." He shook his head.

"They are leaving sooner, so come on, who wants to celebrate?" Sardar cried and held out his hands. His cousins and even a couple of his uncles stood up with Sardar, whooping and dancing around the room.

They were still in the midst of these high-spirited celebrations when the door opened, and Sabir Ali walked in.

"Sahib, there was a call from Aligarh," he said, nodding towards Sardar and Salar. Sardar's family had recently had a telephone installed in the house. "They said to tell you that they expect trouble after the speeches today. The school may not open after the holidays until things are safe again. They said they would inform you of any further developments if they can."

He left the room, leaving behind uneasy silence.

"Even more trouble?" said Sardar.

"How much more?" cried one of his cousins. "People are dying already."

"The violence is restricted to some areas," an aunt reminded them soberly. "They must expect it to spread."

"Jinnah will make sure all is well," said her son confidently.

"Will the *Jamia* be closed too?" Mukhtar asked.

"We should presume it will be," said Riffat Bano.

Sardar dropped wearily into one of the chairs against the wall, his thoughts on the episode in the Punjab Assembly less than three months ago. Master Tara Singh, the Sikh political leader, had drawn his sword and challenged the Muslim League to raise its flag over the Assembly building. It was graphic proof of the public sentiment among many segments of society, which was vehemently against the partition of India. Sardar wondered if there would have been less violence if the leaders agreed to a date for the creation of the new country after the assets had been safely moved to their new home. When he voiced this thought, his uncle shrugged,

"Maybe you're right. It may have made a difference," he said. "Or it may not, we'll never know now, and there is no point wondering about it. It is easier to be wise in hindsight. We need to think ahead; we need to make the right decisions now."

Sardar's father said wearily. "We have to make some sort of a plan if the violence gets out of hand."

His brothers agreed.

A host of questions clamoured for answers in Sardar's mind. If India was divided, would his family move to Pakistan? What would it be like living in a different place, in a home with a different name? His family had never lived anywhere but in Kharkhoda, in India. If they did move then what would become of this house and his family's lands?

The questions went on: Would he ever see Binarsi and Lalli, again? Would he ever see his neighbours again, the families who had lived with them for generations in Kharkhoda? What about the new friends he had made at his current school? Would they all survive whatever lay ahead? What would they do?

He wondered if his Hindu friends had cheered Mountbatten's announcement, but at this, his mouth twisted into a wry smile, as he said out loud, "No." The Hindus were on the brink of losing a large chunk of their country. They would be happy that the British — after almost two hundred years — were leaving India but celebrating Pakistan was a definite no.

Part III

Part III

Syed Sardar Ahmad:

"My family never thought they would have to leave Kharkhoda. Nobody sat down and took the decision to leave the only home they knew. When the violence started on a huge scale, and people from Punjab started moving to Pakistan, it was only then that many others thought it best to leave as well. This was when my family made the decision too.

They left on 9th September as part of a large group of about three or four thousand people. I was not with them. I had left for Delhi and Aligarh by Kalka Mail very early in the morning of 5th September; this is how unprepared we were for what came next. On platform one, where the Kalka Mail was stationed, a huge number …around one hundred and fifty Muslims were killed in front of me on the platform.

Let me tell you, British soldiers were present at the Delhi station when I arrived on 9th September, but they were standing idly by, not moving and not getting involved. The British had stopped getting involved. They just wanted to get out.

I went and sat in the carriage, but I didn't have a ticket to Aligarh. Instead, I had taken a ticket to Mathra because it was the next stop.

So, I was able to reach Aligarh. After I got there, I told the people that they should advise students against commuting to Delhi."

In a woefully mild analogy, Sardar was reminded of one of his writing lessons, which revolved around the words 'Who? What? Where? When? How?' At the brink of the Partition of India, everything was unclear. When would these people know who would go where, what they would be able to carry, and exactly when and how they would leave their homes?

A week from Mountbatten's June Plan, Sardar's family was gathered for the afternoon in the dining room. Temperatures were above 110 Fahrenheit. The doors were closed against the outside heat, and the curtains were drawn to keep out the sun. The fan blades spun in such slow rotations that it was easy to count them. Most of them ate mangoes, which were at their sweetest and best at this time of the year. They were brought to the table on ice; Salar pouted with longing when he saw how cold the mangoes would be.

Sardar's uncles were also present, and after lunch, everyone lingered around the table, waiting for something, nobody was sure what it was that they were waiting for. The room was abnormally quiet and still. Meer Meherbaan Ali sat at the head of the table, his wife by his side. He stared at the glass of *lassi* in his hand, a deep frown on his face. Sardar's father sat beside his mother, his arms on the table, his head bowed over them. His uncles sat next to each other on the other side.

Sardar's three youngest brothers Salar, Iftikhar and little Waqar, usually rowdy, sat quietly at the foot of the table, their eyes darting from one member of the family to the other, amazed at the silence. Sardar sat beside his father with his mother on his other side and Mukhtar next to her, waiting, dreading to hear what he knew was coming…and then it came.

"You need to think about leaving here, *Bhaijan*," Sardar's uncle said.

Sardar heard the sluggish whirring of the fans and a quiet hush fall over the whole of Kharkhoda.

Sharif Ahmad lifted his head, sighed, and lowered it again without responding.

"You said yourself we need a plan if the violence escalates. Well, it is not yet widespread, but I think it will escalate sooner than later. In which case, leaving India and moving to Pakistan is the most obvious plan, the only solution."

"Leaving was not an option I had considered," Sharif Ahmad said heavily, almost to himself. "I was thinking in terms of security around the house or moving someplace temporarily."

His brother pushed his chair back, and stood up, leaning across the table towards his brother. "And what if they burn the house down with all of us in it?" he said quietly.

Sharif Ahmad lifted his head, leant back and folded his arms. "What if they burn us all down while we are 'leaving' as you put it so lightly?" he said.

Riffat Bano leant across Sardar to speak to her husband. "Please. The children are here," she said in a low voice.

"Maybe you should send them out?" Sharif Ahmad suggested, but his wife shook her head.

"No, I don't want to send them away. They have a right to be present when we make decisions that will affect us all."

On the other side of the table, Sardar's uncle took a deep breath before turning to his father.

"*Abba Jan*, it isn't safe to stay here now. India is getting too dangerous for Muslims."

Meer Meherban Ali carried on frowning and said nothing. Sardar's uncle glanced at him before turning towards his sister-in-law, Sardar's mother, hoping for her support.

"*Bhabhijan*, we have jeeps ready to go. Please, just say the word," he said. "Let's leave this place. Please."

Riffat Bano sat quietly, a little away from the table. Her hands rested on her lap, fingers interlaced. Sardar who knew her every habit knew she was not relaxed as the posture would suggest, because of the way her thumbs circled each other, round and round and round. When her brother-in-law spoke to her, her lips tightened almost imperceptibly, and she flicked an invisible speck from her knee.

"How many people will fit into these jeeps that are waiting to take us away?" she said.

Her brother-in-law waved his hand to include them all. "They will take all of us," he said.

"Yes, but can you define 'all of us' for me, please," Riffat Bano pressed.

Sardar's uncle seemed taken aback. "Of course, *Bhabhijan*. I meant all of us, our parents, us brothers," he gestured towards his brothers and himself, "our wives and children. No one will be left out. Leave that to us. Just pick up what you absolutely must take, and let's go."

A young maidservant came in and placed a tea tray in front of Sardar's mother. Riffat Bano thanked her and asked her to bring another cup. When the girl left, Sardar's mother said, "No." She spoke softly, but the single word fell into the quiet room like a gunshot.

"No!" Sardar's uncle cried. "But *why*? How can you refuse, *Bhabhijan*? Surely you haven't thought it through!"

Mukhtar stood up abruptly and standing behind Riffat Bano with a hand on her shoulder, faced his uncle. "My mother never says anything without proper consideration," he said, almost aggressively.

Beseeching her son for speaking out of turn and for the aggression in his tone with a quick shush, Riffat Bano, then, placed a placating hand on his. She turned to address her brother-in-law.

"My decision hinges on your definition of 'all of us,'" she said. Before her brother-in-law could speak again, she handed him his cup of tea, and said, almost conversationally, "That girl who brought in the tea, do you know her name?"

"Her name? Yes, of course, I do," her brother-in-law said. "She's…it's …no, I don't know." He shook his head, impatiently. "But what has that to do with our discussion, *Bhabhijan*? We are talking about the impending danger to our lives." "I too am talking about our lives," she said and held up a hand to stop her brother-in-law from interrupting. "About *all* our lives, which include the lives of our *riaya*, our dependents."

The young girl brought in the extra cup and left again. Riffat Bano started pouring out the tea while she placed a spoon on each saucer.

Her brother-in-law rolled his eyes in frustration and took an impatient turn around the room.

"Come on *Bhabhijan*," he said, coming back to the table. "Look at the greater picture, for God's sake."

His sister-in-law's eyes flashed, and she put down a spoon with a clunk. "Oh, and are *you* looking at the greater picture? That young woman who brought in the tea," she gestured towards the kitchen door, "whose name you do not know, she has been with us since she was nine. You have seen her innumerable times, and she still remains nameless for you, so let me tell you about her. Her mother died of tuberculosis. Before she died, she left her daughter in my charge and begged me to care for her. She does not call me 'mother', but I am the closest to a mother she has. Should I leave her? Should I go away to save myself, when she is in as much danger as we are? Would the dead woman forgive me? Would Allah forgive me?" She lifted up her chin and looked at her brother-in-law, breathing rather fast. "If there is a picture more complete than that, please show it to me. The other people employed by us have worked for us all these years with dedication and honesty only for us to abandon them now? This would be a sad beginning for a country for which we have shed so much blood. Think again, my brother."

Sardar's uncle stared wordlessly at her and then shaking his head, impatiently threw up his hands.

"I am simply thinking of this family," he said to the room at large. "Of our children and our wives. If we start taking everyone along…surely there are too many of them."

"I know you are thinking of our families," Sardar's father spoke then, gently. "I know you, my brother. You are a good man. But I agree with my wife. We have to leave together, or not at all."

Sardar's uncle turned to his father, who had been silent all this time. "*Abba Jan*! Make him understand what is at stake!"

He turned furiously to the brothers. "Speak!" he cried. "Why are you silent? Say something! Why am I left standing here all alone?"

Sardar's grandfather smiled sadly. "Sit down, my son. Sit down." He waited while his son seated himself again, very reluctantly.

"You are not alone," Meer Meherbaan Ali said, "This is a family counsel." He took a deep breath. "I understand what you are saying, but I think your brother Sharif Ahmad and Riffat *beti* understand much better what is at stake," he said. "We have sacrificed before, if fate decrees another sacrifice of our family, then so be it, Allah have Mercy on us all." He turned to his younger sons sitting together on one side of the table. "Think again, my sons," he said. "This is our home, the home of our ancestors; our home has been under attack before, but that does not mean we abandon it. Is leaving a piece of yourself, right?"

Sardar's uncles all appeared to have lost their voice. Then the uncle who had spoken earlier nodded and sighed. "*Bhabhijan* is right, of course," he said. "I allowed my fears to cloud my judgement and my honour. I am sorry, *Bhabhijan*," he inclined his head towards her. "We will work something out, so we can all go together."

That was the end of the argument.

The independence of Pakistan was announced through Radio Pakistan on August 13, 1947, at 11:59 p.m. in Urdu, followed by announcements in Urdu and English by Mustafa Ali Hamdani, "Greetings! Pakistan Broadcasting Service. We are speaking from Lahore, the night between the thirteen and fourteen of August, year forty-seven. It is twelve o'clock, the Dawn of Freedom."

On the 14th of August 1947, Mountbatten administered the oath of office to Jinnah in Karachi, and the dignified lawyer became the first Governor-General of Pakistan.

India and Pakistan came into being as two separate countries at the stroke of midnight between the 14th and 15th of August 1947. At the moment of Independence, the air was filled with the sound of whistles, hooters and conch shells, and then the death and destruction escalated to unimaginable levels.

In Punjab on the West, and Bengal on the East, there was more violence than anywhere else. Entire caravans of migrants were massacred, trains setting out from one side often arrived at the other with the occupants slain, decapitated, dismembered. People described blood dripping from the carriages as they ground to a halt at the station and the cries of those whose dear ones had been killed before their eyes. Women were raped and murdered, and unborn children ripped out of their mother's bellies. These atrocities were not committed by any one community; the genocide occurred across the board.

Refugee camps were set up at various points and were so overcrowded that disease spread like wildfire in them.

What was a mere debate in Sardar's family months back was now swaying towards a very clear direction. The news of violence became frequent; as the details became horrific, the enthusiasm for staying back and defending their home started to dwindle.

The intention to migrate strengthened. Sharif Ahmad suggested that they initiate dialogue with the Hindu and Sikh *zamindars* whose lands were falling within the territory now known as Pakistan. This dialogue would entail an exchange of land; a Hindu family would move here, and they would move there.

They decided that they would leave as a large group, together with others moving from the neighbourhood, hoping for safety in numbers. Meantime, they would make what arrangements were required.

"It will be a huge group," Sardar's grandfather warned. "It will be larger than we realise now."

Sardar's father shrugged, "So be it."

Sardar had been silent throughout the conversation. His heart quailed at the entirely possible tragic culmination of their plans.

The mass migration that followed August 14th had not been encapsulated; the general perception was that India would be declared as two independent states, and that is all there will be to it. The commoner had not envisioned being uprooted from their homes as they were. The process of migration from this side to that began as fear gripped the sub-continent. There were riots, violence, death and destruction, more in some parts of the country than in others and much more was expected the moment the British left. The people of India braced themselves for that day, tense and fearful.

As each new report came to their attention, the family in Kharkhoda prayed even harder than before that their own exodus would not end in tragedy. It was as Sardar's aunt reminded herself as she went about packing the pitifully few possessions they were able to take with them, "All decisions rest with Allah."

"Things, these are just things," Sardar's mother muttered all day like it was a self-placating mantra.

They wondered how other people were handling their belongings and how they had managed to solve the problem of what to take and what to leave behind.

"After all, we need *some* things to survive," Sardar's aunt said feverishly, several times a day. "Money, clothes, food, furniture..."

One of their neighbours, an elderly man and a close friend of the family, dug a pit in his garden into which he buried a box in the middle of the night. Sardar and his father knew about it because they were asked to help. The neighbour's sons were dead, his grandsons were too young, and he did not want to entrust anyone else with the task because, as he confided in them, gold is too heavy to take with us, nor is it safe to carry it around. One day my grandsons will come back and dig it up again," he said confidently. "I will tell them where it is. After all, this mess cannot last forever."

Sardar's father said nothing as he replaced earth over the pit with Sardar's help, and covered it again with turf as best as he could.

Another couple Sardar's parents knew, did not want to leave Kharkhoda because their child was buried in the local graveyard.

"There is nothing I can say to persuade them to change their mind," Sardar's mother said tearfully, one of the very few occasions he had seen her break down.

Home had always been a safe haven. Home had always been the familiar sights and sounds of Kharkhoda. Knowing he was being unreasonable, Sardar could not help wishing they could stay back; if they could only just stay there, very quietly, maybe they would be safe. Whenever this longing tugged at him, he reminded himself sternly that it was time to abandon such childish ideas.

Schools and colleges had been closed since Mountbatten's announcement.

Riffat Bano's brother Professor Khwaja Manzoor, chairman of the English Department, Aligarh, had sent his son to visit family in Kharkhoda for the summers. Despite not hearing from her brother, Sardar's mother told her nephew to leave for Delhi. "They may not have been able to phone in this confusion," she said. "Lines have been down all over, including, it seems, theirs. Go to Delhi; we cannot be sure if *Bhaijan* Manzoor is in Aligarh, hence it is safer to go to *Qamar Manzil*. Sardar will go with you. Both of you should be safe there, *In Sha Allah*. I beg to God for your safety."

She could sense Sardar's apprehension, "Leave for Pakistan with your aunt and uncle whenever they do themselves. Meantime we will leave from here, and *In Sha Allah,* we should be safe as well." Sardar knew she was putting up a brave front for his sake.

"But why should I go to Delhi when you're all leaving from here?" he protested.

"I do not wish to put all my treasures in the same basket, my dearest," Riffat Bano said with an attempt at a smile. "I want you to take your cousin to Delhi to his parents. Mukhtar is very impetuous. The others are still too young." She stood up. "So that is settled then. In a few days, you leave for Delhi. May Allah be with you."

To his ears, she sounded confident, although he knew otherwise. She kissed him, and he did not see her shut her eyes as soon as she turned away and hold on to a chair back to steady herself. He only saw her walk out of the room with steady steps.

Sardar did not wish to leave his family. He wanted to stay in Kharkhoda and go with them whenever they left. When he said this and expressed his fears for their safety, his grandfather placed his hand on Sardar's head.

"May Allah keep you in His care, my child," he said. "And all of us as well. Go as your mother says. You should be safe in Delhi, and *In Sha Allah,* we will be heading towards Delhi in such large numbers that it should be safe for us to travel as well. Once we reach Delhi, then we make plans for crossing the border."

"Where exactly is this border?" blurted Sardar.

His grandfather shrugged. "The Boundary Commission settled on the boundaries just before the British left, but the decision was published only a few days ago. Your father has read it. He and his brothers wish to head for the city of Lahore which is not too far from here. You will be going there with Manzoor and others." He sighed. "India…cut into pieces! I never thought I would see such a thing."

Striving for a less depressing note, he added, "It turns out we will be part of a group of three or four thousand."

"Ma Sha Allah!" Sardar was startled. "How can there be so many of you?"

"Ma Sha Allah we're a large family, we are all of Kharkhoda," said Sardar's grandfather. "Most of the Muslims from around here have decided to leave. We will all go together. There's safety in numbers."

Sardar felt sick to the heart when he said goodbye to his family very early on the 9th of September. The furniture was still in place, the books still on their shelves, the pictures where they had always been on the walls. The sense of belonging that had permeated these walls seemed to be missing as agitation towards departure built up.

His father gave him some documents as he was leaving. "These are your identity documents," he said. "Keep them with you at all times," he stressed the last three words.

Then Sardar left the house with his cousin to catch the Kalka Mail to Delhi. He dropped off his cousin in Delhi and decided to continue all the way to Aligarh to check in on *Mamu Jan* Manzoor.

There were people on both sides of the platform at the Delhi train station, passengers and porters carrying luggage and pushing trolleys, cleaners with brooms, and vendors selling tea and breakfast, a painful satire upon normalcy that was confined to this moment in time.

Sardar rejected one bench because it was broken, another because it was wet and had just sat down with a book upon the third when he heard shouts, desperate screams, and the sound of frantically running feet. Getting to his feet quickly, he looked around, panic-stricken, for the source of the noise. What he saw froze his blood. Where there had been nothing but men, women and children ambling along a few minutes ago, now several people lay in a pool of blood on the other platform. Their lives extinguished in the few seconds that Sardar's attention had been focused on finding a place to sit.

Right across him on that same platform, a group of men surrounded a woman and grabbed her child. Sardar stared horrified as the woman screamed, trying to pull her child away.

"Ya Allah!" she shouted, "*Choro meri bachi ko, chor do*! Leave my child! Leave her alone!"

One of the men pulled out a knife and stabbed the woman.

Sardar's shout was drowned out by the child's terrified screams as the men stabbed the child as well.

On that platform now, people lay dead in the midst of trunks and bundles, their contents scattered everywhere. The walls and the platform were splashed with blood.

A couple of men ran up and down, looking like fiends greedy to kill.

Sardar's heart thumped frantically in his chest. Along with other passengers, he backed further and further away from the bloody scene, finally reaching the end of his platform. Safety in numbers, his grandfather had said…safety in numbers, the old man had insisted. He desperately tried to figure out the best thing to do, which was to board the train that would take him away from this horror. It was due any minute now, to his immense relief, he heard the train approaching. As he was scrambling up its steps, he saw some British soldiers on the platform.

The British soldiers, in their khaki uniforms and pith helmets, belted, booted and armed, stood not far from where so many people lay dead, facing purposefully away from the carnage. They were doing nothing to help the victims or apprehend the killers from getting away. Sardar's emotions threatened to choke him, and anger pulsed through his veins.

"It was your war we fought, your war we died in, you *farangis*," he hissed at them, his hand clenching on the handrails. "Get out of here now, why don't you? Get out!" He strode into the train and threw his luggage violently onto the rack. As the train picked up speed, the wheels seemed to spit out the words "Get out! Get out!" faster and faster until his head felt like exploding.

Sardar bought a ticket for Mathra, the stop after Aligarh. Mathra was predominantly Hindu. He felt it would be safer to be seen going there rather than to the predominantly Muslim Aligarh. He got off at Aligarh of course, thanking God for being alive.

Aligarh University was open, serving the higher cause of Education as Sir Syed would have wanted.

As soon as he got there, Sardar told the school secretary what had occurred on the Delhi train station. As he walked to the office and out again, as he went to his dorm and took a bath, as he put his things away and joined his fellow students in the common room, and later that night as he tried to sleep, Sardar found he could think of little else but the scene he had witnessed on the railway platform. The people's screams and the screams of the little girl and her mother followed him everywhere. He found out later that a hundred and fifty people died on Platform One that morning.

This should have been the beginning of Sardar's second year of College, his intermediate year of studying Commerce.

12th October, 2016

Syed Sardar Ahmad:

"In Aligarh, the lava of resentment was building up inside, but there was peace on the surface. There were no violent incidents in Aligarh. My *Mamu Jan*, Khwaja Manzoor Hosain was in Aligarh. He was a professor at the university and the chairman of the English Department. I was staying with him.

My maternal aunt's husband, my *khalu*, Z. A. Hashmi Sahib, who became Karachi's Collector later on, was staying in Agra City. He sent a car to pick me up, but he didn't say we were leaving for Pakistan. Everything was done quietly; the luggage was packed secretly. We sat in that car and went to Agra. Then all of us, my *khalu* — and his children, we took all our luggage and boarded a train. It was a military special which was leaving from Agra for Lahore and Rawalpindi in Pakistan.

The only men on the train with us were military men. These men were with the army and had opted for Pakistan. There were a few other civilians. All the people on the train were Muslims.

We saw dead bodies on both sides of the train tracks after Patiala. Dogs and vultures were picking on them.

At the stations we passed, we could see train carriages carrying Muslim refugees. At some, there were one or two, at others, there were three or more carriages. These carriages had been standing there for the past few days, and their food and water supply was blocked. It seemed likely that these people would be martyred during the journey. We made attempts to hook these carriages along with our train, but we were warned that it was none of our business.

It took two days for this military special to reach Lahore. On 24th September, I was at the Lahore station. From the day I left Kharkhoda, it took me 19 days to reach Lahore. Once in Lahore, I came to know that all the passengers of those other carriages we had seen had been killed, they were martyred. Not a single train arrived unharmed.**"**

Sardar stood at an arched window in one of the corridors at Aligarh, looking out onto the grounds. There on his left were the beds of red roses and yellow daffodils that his mother had admired so much on her visit to Aligarh. On the right was the *neem* tree under which Mukhtar used to sit, reading or talking to a friend or just lost deep in thought.

Home. The word held an echo now that it had not contained before, as if the word was reaching out to him from the depths of a dark tunnel, empty. He shook himself, trying to pull himself out of this wretched mood. Here he was, in Aligarh, in college, safe with others his age and his teachers. He must trust in God to take care of his family.

Yet there was little doubt about it, Aligarh felt unreal now. Its halls and corridors were no longer noisy. Where students once dodged each other laughing and shouting as they raced to their classes or meals, there was now only the sound of the past being severed from the present.

Aligarh's graceful buildings and manicured lawns — still impeccable were now even more at odds with the real world which was nothing but chaos and anger. People, uprooted from their homes, lost in wounds and gore, walking through an unmourned bloodbath.

The University was in financial trouble. In the last couple of years, the government had cut down its grants drastically, as had the princely states. Many of its students had left for Pakistan, and enrolment was falling day by day. Several of Sardar's friends were no longer there. Students had not returned because of political trouble. Most of the staff had migrated to Pakistan. The Vice-Chancellor Zahid Husain stayed back to fulfil his commitment to education until he was asked to leave. The University was temporarily looked after by a local landlord, *Janab* Obaidur Rahman Sherwani, who was also a member of the UP legislative assembly.

After he returned to Aligarh, Sardar and his fellow students ventured into the streets a couple of times. They saw shutters pulled down on stores; several had new owners because the previous ones had either sold their businesses or their businesses had been forcibly taken away from them.

They saw groups of exhausted persons walking down the road on their way to Pakistan or coming from there. They had bundles and bags on their heads, goats, crying children, and elderly persons on carts in tow. Once they saw, someone throw a stone at such a group. It hit a woman who collapsed in the dust with a hoarse cry.

A truck of British soldiers appeared around a bend in the road and disappeared in a cloud of dust down the street.

"They came, and they went," a boy next to Sardar had

muttered, following the truck with narrowed eyes. "Leaving us breathing the dust they raised."

Sardar shivered. "When will this stop?" he whispered and turned away from the window looking onto the garden. The corridor behind him was silent. From behind the screen door of one of the classrooms came the low drone of someone reading out loud, and the scrape of a chair being pushed back. From the clock tower, the hour struck three.

Yes, there was no violence at Aligarh, but the prevailing tranquillity felt frail. There were cracks in this peace through which fear and anger came bubbling out like lava.

If any of them received a phone call or a telegram, it was a moment of terror. It could mean bad news. Sardar himself had heard nothing from his family since he left. All he knew was that they too had left home. Sardar could not help wonder about his family often, fervently hoping they were safe.

His father had asked him not to worry, "God only knows how long it will take us to get from one place to another. Not all places have phones, and both mail and phone lines are disrupted these days."

Sardar was now even more glad than usual that *Mamu Jan* Manzoor, was in Aligarh. Sardar saw him frequently at school because he taught English there and headed the English Department; he had always liked visiting his family. However, before the riots and trouble started, he would not have wished to leave the company of his friends at the hostel and live anywhere else. Now, after Sardar returned to Aligarh, his uncle said, "I think it is best if you leave the hostel and stay with us," Sardar complied feeling immeasurable relief.

His mother's sister, on the other hand, lived in Agra city with her husband, Z. A. Hashmi, and their children. The plan was to leave for Pakistan soon, and Sardar was to go with them.

Mamu Jan Manzoor and his family would follow a bit later from Aligarh.

Late in September 1947, twelve days after he had returned to Aligarh, a car sent by *Khalu Jan* Hashmi arrived at Manzoor Hosain's house. Sardar said goodbye to his uncle, praying he would see them soon. He got into the car as if he was going to the shops with a discreet little bag containing just a few possessions. He knew he was leaving home; he knew he was going to Agra in this car, and he knew he was leaving India for good. Would this Pakistan be home one day? Would he survive to see his family again? He did not know.

He said goodbye in his heart to every stone he passed, to the cinema, to the shop where they used to buy their stationery, the bakery they bought the occasional cake from. He asked every bird to carry his love to his family — wherever his family was.

There were discreet signs of packing at the Hashmi home. It was not possible to be open about it because people had been murdered just to prevent them from leaving. Small bundles and bags — they could not take much, were tucked away where no outsider was likely to see them.

The next day all these bundles and bags were placed into the car as secretly as possible.

"Do you have your identity documents?" his uncle confirmed from Sardar. All of them, his aunt and uncle and their two small children squeezed into the small Volkswagen with Sardar, and they drove off down the streets of Agra.

They passed the Taj Mahal, to Sardar's overwrought imagination the Mahal looked like a woman brought to her knees by grief.

In silence, they reached the Agra railway station. Men in army uniform swiftly and silently loaded their things and helped them climb on board a special train, moving military personnel who had opted for Pakistan. There were a few other civilian families as well besides them. The train was full to its maximum capacity.

"Where are we going?" Sardar's small cousin kept asking. "Is it a long trip, *Ammijee*?" his mother tried to distract him, but he wouldn't stop.

"We always go for many days when we take a train!" he fretted. "Why didn't you tell me? I should have brought *Munni* with me!" *Munni* was his cat. He fretted about who would feed his cat until the train gave a great jolt and only then was he diverted.

They were leaving, puffing out of the station, out of Agra, out of India and headed for Lahore. It was the 22nd of September 1947.

It was noisy on the train, the sound of children, crying, playing, shouting, and talking. The elders spoke in low voices when they spoke at all, blinking away their tears trying to keep fear and despair at bay. Outside, the countryside turned greener, more fields, more trees, and increasingly more carnage as they travelled towards the newly created border between India and Pakistan. There were no birds chirping hope. There were vultures and crows circling the skies over bodies on either side of the tracks. There were dogs sniffing on the corpses, feeding on the men, women and children who had died in an attempt to escape the violence that was encapsulating the country. Sardar felt as if the lump in his throat would never go away. Was this freedom?

Halfway to Delhi, they passed a train on one of the tracks parallel to theirs. The carriages were charred and burnt. Their train moved on, passing more dead bodies beside the tracks, at times just severed arms or legs.

When they were almost at Delhi, they saw another train which did not appear damaged, but it was not moving. Its stranded passengers sat or stood beside it. Some had their prayer mats spread out on the muddy ground, praying for safety. Seeing a train approach a few men ran towards the tracks and tried to flag it down, pleading to be rescued. A few fathers held out their children begging the passengers to have mercy on these innocent souls, asking their children to be given safe passage in the train. The passengers stared back at them, full of horror at being unable to stop and help.

"Can't we stop and take those people with us?" Sardar asked his uncle, urgently. But his uncle shook his head.

"I asked," he said helplessly, "The captain said it was his responsibility to get us across without loss of life, he has strict orders to not stop on the way."

There were several train stations on the way to Lahore — New Delhi, Ludhiana, and Atari, but they didn't plan to stop at any of them.

Delhi drew closer. The passengers clustered around the windows to catch a glimpse of the capital of India. Sardar's thoughts kept wandering off to his family. He buried his face in his hands for a moment, praying that all was well with them.

They could see the buildings of Delhi now, as well as a dark plume of smoke.

"What's happened there, *Bhai*?" said Sardar's cousin. "We're going straight towards the smoke."

"I don't know," Sardar shook his head. "The train will stop if it has to, don't worry."

The train kept going as they drew even closer to the smoke.

"We're going into the fire!" a little girl cried. "We'll be burnt! Stop the train!"

The train moved on relentlessly towards a smoke-lined horizon; there were buildings on fire. It was not until they were very close to them did the tracks curve to the right. Smoke filled the carriages. Coughing, gasping and wiping their streaming eyes the people around the windows saw charred bricks and burning pieces of wood scattered everywhere. Men were throwing buckets of water into the fire.

Eyes streaming, the passengers stared at the scene they were passing through. People were standing in the rubble despite the fire and choking pollution. A couple of men walked by carrying a body between them, and a line of people straggled behind, crying and holding on to each other. The train moved on.

Delhi had drawn even closer when they heard the sound of running feet. There was chaos, people calling urgently to one another, screams of women and children shrieked.

They were welcomed with shots fired at the train, a rat-a-tat volley that made the passengers crouch to the floor and cover their ears. A few shots hit the train, something somewhere fell with a crash, and people screamed. The Delhi station, the same red building, the same arches and turrets edged with white, where Sardar and his brothers had stopped so often on their way to school.

These platforms were once crowded with students. Coolies used to step briskly through the crowd carrying bedding rolls and suitcases, and vendors held out their wares hopefully to tired passengers. Now, the platform was spilling over with terrified people — exhausted, desperate, frustrated and angry. They scurried after the moving train, tried to mount it, to stop it, but the train driver was determined to continue along without slowing down.

"Put down the windows!" an army Captain bellowed, running

through the train. "Hurry!"

"This one is stuck!" shouted a soldier from one of the compartments near theirs. The captain went running into that compartment, and together the two men tried to pull down the glass which was all the way up. It would not budge, leaving the people inside dangerously exposed. The two men sent them all out, grunting as they struggled with the window.

Screams filled the air as people threw themselves at the train. The train shook from side to side.

At that moment, something flew through the open window towards the two men. Both ducked, but it hit the soldier who had first tried to pull down the glass. He fell down, and they just managed to hear a woman scream: "Look after him! For the sake of Allah! He is…"

The woman's voice receded with every word as the train moved on, its whistle drowning out the rest.

When the Captain turned, he found his companion on the floor, a small child on his chest, a boy, about two years old. Each was staring at the other, flabbergasted.

The Captain picked the little boy off the soldier's chest, and the child burst into screams. He squirmed out of the man's arms and threw himself onto the ground where he continued screaming, bringing other soldiers into the carriage.

"Captain, do you think we could…" the soldier began, but the Captain shook his head very firmly.

"Not to mention that we would all die in the attempt," the Captain said drily, and reluctantly the man agreed that going back would not help.

The soldier's wife looked after the boy all the way to Lahore. "Poor, poor little one," she said. "God only knows what is going through his mind; what he has already gone through."

She tried to stroke the child's face, but that resulted in a renewed bout of screams, so she drew back.

He calmed down after a bit, enough to eat a mouthful or two, then cowered on his seat, sniffing, as if afraid of being hit. The recent welter of emotions had exhausted him, but every time his eyes closed, he jerked himself awake again. Eventually, his thick eyelashes come to rest on his cheeks, and he stopped whimpering. His snores when they came were tiny defiant sounds that each ended in a little whistle.

Sardar's aunt came to sit beside the soldier's wife and the little boy. The two women smiled sadly when the whistles became strident. Sardar's aunt reached out to lightly touch the boy's still chubby feet. "What are we going to do about him," she said desperately, "when…?" She left a lot more hanging in the air.

The soldier upon whom the child had fallen took a deep breath. "I've been thinking about that," he began tentatively, looking at his wife. "It will depend upon you of course," he said, addressing her, "but maybe we could…"

His wife nodded. "Allah will help us," she said. "We have two of our own; we may as well have a third."

Her husband smiled gratefully at her. "Thank you," he said. "I feel as if this happened for a reason."

His wife nodded. "Yes. I wish we knew his name. If he doesn't tell us, we can give him my brother's name," she said softly.

"My brother-in-law was killed last month," the soldier explained to Sardar's aunt. "He was out buying grocery."

They were just a few miles away from Ludhiana the next day when there was a screech of brakes and the train ground to a halt. Everyone looked out of the windows, wondering if they had been forced to stop, but there was no discernible reason to. Two soldiers stepped out to check, and then the firing began. They ducked instinctively, ran ahead, still crouched, picked up something and tossed it to one side. It was a large log of wood that had been blocking the tracks. They were about to return to the train when there was another round of firing, the one in the lead fell down just beside the door that was being held open for them. There was a shriek as the man's wife tried to run out, but the other women held her back. The other soldier pulled her husband into the train with help from those inside. The train was already moving; they slammed the door shut and hauled the man who had been shot into the passage.

"He's dead," grunted the other soldier. There was a shocked intake of breath, and the man's family burst into tears. People could be heard muttering "*Inna llillahi wa inna ilayhi raji'un* — Indeed, to Allah, we belong, and to Allah, we return." The small boy who had been thrown into the train started screaming again.

As the men bent down to pick up the soldier to carry him into a compartment, there was a loud 'wheeee' and an explosion from somewhere behind them. The train shook violently. The men who were bending down to lift up their *shaheed* colleague fell onto the floor; one of them hit his head hard against a sliding door. The loaded rifle he was carrying went off, shattering the glass on one of the carriage doors.

A shard hit Sardar on the forehead. Sardar's aunt, who had herself fallen down picked herself off the floor and rushed to him. She brought a mug of water and dabbed at the blood with her dupatta.

"It isn't very deep," she said. "Thank God."

"It's just a slight cut, *Khala*," he whispered. "I am okay."

Sardar looked out of the window and just managed to catch sight of the sign for Ludhiana station. It was a smaller station than Delhi's.

They saw another train at a standstill here. Men were pushing against it, trying to shove it off the tracks. They could see terrified faces looking out the train's windows and heard raucous cries and shouts from the men outside.

Crowds gathered beside their train at Ludhiana station, as they had in Delhi, shouting for the train to stop. People tried to hold on to the train, some tried to climb on top of it, and several succeeded. The people inside saw heels disappearing up the windows and heard footsteps on the roof.

"Let them stay," the Captain said curtly when a soldier looked questioningly at him.

"We don't know if they're friend or foe," the soldier said, looking upwards at the ceiling.

The Captain shrugged. "That's why we don't want to pull them in," he said. "But they can stay up there. Just make sure all the windows are down and the doors well locked."

Nothing happened though. The people on the roof seemed to have made themselves as comfortable as they could in the blazing sun. Sardar hoped they had water to drink.

They reached Atari that evening. There, once again, men ran beside the train banging on whichever part of it they could reach to make it stop. More people climbed up on the roof and joined those already there. The train carried on as before, and that evening, on the 24th of September, it crossed the border near Amritsar into Pakistan. The passengers fell to their knees in gratitude, and only stood up when the train pulled up at the station in Lahore, right in front of a sign that said 'Lahore' in English, Urdu and Hindi, but someone had scribbled across the Hindi with a very rough hand.

Sardar's thoughts had been with his parents, and the rest of his family, he wondered where and how they were. As they picked up their things, thanked the soldiers who had looked after them and disembarked onto the platform, he fretted about his family, and about the stranded people they had passed along the way.

They learnt later that most of them had been massacred.

13th October, 2016

Syed Sardar Ahmad:

"I got news of my family from someone we knew from our visits to Barotha, near Attock in Punjab. She read about my family in the newspaper and told us.

We knew Mian Iftikhar-ud-Din, the Minister for the Rehabilitation of Refugees in Pakistan at that time. He called Rohtak's administration to confirm the information. He was told that members of my family had formed a caravan and left for Pakistan, but that they didn't have any more information than this.

One of our relatives lived in Rohtak, and I thought that maybe some of the family might have gone there. Although I had already been told that my family had not survived, there was this hope that someone might have survived. So, I requested Mian Iftikhar-ud-Din for one or two trucks, to rescue any relatives who were stuck there. If any of them were still alive, I wanted to bring them safely to Pakistan. Mian Iftikhar was very generous and gave me the trucks, and based on this hope, I left for India.

On the way, I saw Sabir Ali. He recognised me and called out to me, but the soldier driving the truck said that we were not allowed to stop. We kept going. Well, at least he knew that I was alive...Sabir knew.

We arrived at Rohtak. I was able to bring many people back in the trucks from Rohtak. My aunt who lived next door to my parents, in the same village as my family, she was married to my father's brother Aziz Sahib, they were in Rohtak too. There was fear that women might be raped in case of an attack, so these people had left Kharkhoda and moved to Rohtak. I was able to bring her to Pakistan along with her mother and their extended families, and my father's cousin and his wife, and her brothers' and their families. We filled both trucks to full capacity.**"**

It is not easy to embrace a new life while the old one remains as uncertain as Sardar's was. Hardly a moment went by that he did not think of his parents, his grandparents, and his brothers. He continuously wondered if they were alive, he prayed with all his heart that they were. He wondered what Mukhtar thought of what was happening, how Salar and the younger two were coping. He missed his parents. Oh, how he missed his parents!

His relatives did everything they could to help to find out how the family in Kharkhoda had fared, but there was no news of them. Sardar checked refugee camps for any sign of his family. A few days after they reached Lahore, a headmistress at a school in Barotha, rang his aunt. She was aware of the situation and had heard something that might be relevant.

"There is news about the massacre of a large group of people near Kharkhoda," she said hesitantly. "I wonder if…if God forbid, there is any connection…?"

His aunt could hardly bring herself to pass on the question to her nephew, but she did.

Sardar paled when he heard what she had to say. If someone were to ask him to identify the most important thing Partition had taught him personally, he would say it was the ability to push his worries firmly into some dark recess of his mind and carry on living. He did so now, grasping on to the hope that perhaps it was some other group his aunt's friend had heard about, not the one his family was part of. Perhaps his family had managed to reach safety, and they were trying to get in touch.

Mian Iftikharuddin owned and operated the newspaper Pakistan Times, one of the major newspapers in Pakistan. He had once been a member of the Indian National Congress but had moved to the Pakistan Muslim League in 1946. In 1947, after Partition, he was appointed a Minister in the Punjab Government; his portfolio was the Rehabilitation of Refugees. Sardar's uncle Z. A Hashmi knew him and enlisted his help.

Mian Iftikharuddin phoned some people he knew in the local government at Rohtak, which was not far from Kharkhoda.

"The families you speak of left Kharkhoda. This is all the information we have," he was told.

It was not conclusive, and that tiny sliver of hope remained.

Sardar went to see Mian Iftikharuddin himself.

"I cannot rest unless I know where my family is, I need to know if they are alive or not," he said, sitting across Mian Iftikharuddin in his office in Lahore. His voice came close to breaking, and he brought it sternly under control.

"I want to go to Rohtak to see what I can find. I know trucks are being sent to India for those who want to migrate to Pakistan. I want to ride with one of the trucks to Kharkhoda; I will try to find my relatives and bring back whoever is still alive, if…if any of them are still alive."

Sardar set out on this quest to find his family accompanied by a couple of trucks, driven by soldiers. He left for Rohtak, which was some twenty-five miles from Kharkhoda. They were among thousands of people leaving Pakistan on foot, by car or cart. Coming the other way was a similar tide of people moving to Pakistan. Sardar searched for his family in every exhausted group, he saw a brother in every young man, and he saw glimpses of his mother in every mother he passed on the way. Once he saw an old man who walked just like his grandfather and his heart lurched within his chest, but it was not his *Dadajan*. At another time he thought he saw a slim boy who walked with the same flat-footed gait as Salar. But it was a girl. She had probably dressed as a boy to escape attention but had not succeeded in disguising herself well enough.

They drove past an old woman limping towards the border on the arm of a young man, and several groups carrying the sick or elderly on charpoys. Sardar was not allowed to help anyone. The soldiers would not stop. They had orders not to get involved in anything other than taking Sardar to Rohtak, find refugees there and bring them back.

"Where did your people come from?" Sardar asked the soldier who was driving the truck he was in. "Have you always lived in Lahore?"

The man grunted. "We're from Shimla," he said. "In India."

"What did your parents do there?"

"They ran a rest-house," the man said. "British officers used to come and stay there in summer."

"Are your parents in Lahore now?"

"They're dead," the man said baldly. "They were killed."

They had a long road ahead of them. They would stop at obscure places for meals when darkness fell; they would drive into a copse of trees to conceal the vehicles as best as possible so the soldiers could take turns to rest.

It was about four days later that in the midst of a group of people crossing the road in front of their truck, Sardar recognised one person, a tall man with long moustaches that curled upwards. Sardar's heart gave a great leap as he realised it was Sabir Ali.

"Stop! Stop!" Sardar shouted. The driver of his truck jammed on the brakes automatically, thinking perhaps they were about to hit something. When he heard the screech of brakes, Sabir Ali glanced at their truck. His eyes lit up when he saw Sardar leaning out of the window, waving, but the truck had already moved on.

"Don't do that again," the soldier scolded, pulling Sardar back into the cabin. Sardar begged him to go back or stop, but he refused. "We cannot stop here; the officials will just ask us to go back the way we came. Did you not see the army officials on the other side of the road? The man you saw is being escorted safely to Pakistan; you need not worry about him."

Sardar slewed around in his seat. He saw Sabir Ali pushing through the people around him, stopping in frustration by the side of the road, his hands on his hips as he saw the truck moving down the road again.

Sardar tried to plead with his driver, told him whom he had seen, but the man would not listen to him. Sardar had to give up. It was probably the hardest thing he had ever done, but he had promised Mian Iftikharuddin he would obey the soldiers.

Sardar reminded himself that Sabir Ali had seen him too. Sardar knew Sabir Ali well enough to be sure he would search for him, now that he knew that he, Sardar, was alive. It was therefore with a less heavy heart, despite the likelihood of the worst news at the other end that Sardar carried on towards Rohtak.

The sun was setting when they reached Rohtak. At a deserted crossroad, they stopped to debate which way to go.

"I think it is better if both trucks don't turn up at your family's house at the same time," said the other soldier, leaning in at the window of their truck. "I've seen people look curiously at us several times and I don't want to draw more attention than is necessary. I'll park in that empty space, besides the shop," he pointed to a store. "People won't worry about a truck being there. They'll think it's making a delivery or something. You go on."

"All right then," the soldier driving Sardar's truck agreed. "We'll come back to you."

Sardar tried to recollect which way he had to go, "We have to turn right at a small *mandir*," he said hesitantly. "Then there's a school somewhere, and the house is behind that." The driver looked about him. "I can't see a school or a *mandir* here."

"I might recognise something," said Sardar, even though nothing looked familiar as yet.

He had visited relatives in Rohtak. Now, he looked all around. Several houses on one side were down to rubble. On the road going the other side, a large bull lay in the middle of the road and did not seem disposed to move. A third road had been dug up.

They drove down the only other road to locate the *mandir* or school but could not find either, nor did they wish to draw attention to themselves by asking. Nothing he saw seemed familiar to Sardar until they came to a small well.

"Wait!' he laid an urgent hand on the soldier's arm and pointed to the well. "I remember that well. They put *that*," he pointed to a rusted metal fence going around the edge of the well, "to prevent animals from falling in."

He got out of the truck and turned this way and that, trying to orient himself, muttering under his breath. Finally, he seemed to have made up his mind and climbed back into the truck.

"That way," he said excitedly, pointing to the left. "I think I remember my father taking us down there, after we left the well."

The driver turned as directed.

"There should be....there it is!" Sardar pointed to a decrepit gate of a school. "We found it! The temple is probably on that side," he indicated ahead of them. "We might have seen it first if we'd come the other way. Let's go behind this school."

The driver did as he was told, and Sardar spotted the house. "That's it," he said excitedly. "That's the house! I recognise the gate!"

It was a red brick house with an elaborately scrolled black iron gate that came to a high peak in the centre.

"*Alhamdulillah*," muttered the driver under his breath. "I didn't expect to find it at all." He parked across the street. "What do you want to do now?"

"Let me go in and check," Sardar said, opening his door.

"No, you stay," the soldier said firmly. "I'll go." He tucked his pistol discreetly into his pocket, opened the gate and walked up the driveway.

Sardar opened his door again and followed him. "I don't see why he should get himself killed in order to save me," he muttered to himself.

The soldier frowned when Sardar walked up beside him just as the door opened a crack, and a woman looked out. It was Riffat Bano's cousin, older but definitely her.

"*Khala Jan*?" said Sardar, his voice unsteady. "I'm Sardar, Riffat Bano's son."

There were eleven people in the house.

They were all stunned to see him and clustered around, asking him how he had got there, what news he had. He told them as briefly as he could because his story was too painful, but also because he needed — more desperately than he could explain — to hear what news they had of his family.

"*Beta*, my husband was afraid we women would be dishonoured," said one woman, on the verge of tears. "That is why we came here, we left with so much of our family still in Kharkhoda, and…and we heard…"

Sardar looked steadily at her, his heart pleading with her not to tell him the worst, but she told Sardar as gently as she could that they had heard his immediate family had not survived.

"You…you can't go to Kharkhoda, Sardar," she said. "Those people are still looking for more to prey at. It is hard to stop when once you…" She covered her face with her hands and wept. "Pray, just pray. It's all we can do for our family."

Another man spoke up to warn him as well, "I heard that the *Jats* from the surrounding villages are still hungry for Muslim blood" he said. "Going to Kharkhoda is no less than suicide."

He went on to confirm Sardar's worst fears, "I have heard specifically that Meer Meherbaan Ali died, his family with him," he told Sardar gently. "No one wishes to believe it, but the news seems very likely to be true," he said. "Only Allah knows the truth."

At a time like this, it was best to put one's own grief aside and focus on someone else's.

"I hope the reports are wrong," Sardar held his weeping aunt in his arms, even though his own eyes were drenched with tears. "Whether they are right or wrong, I know you should all leave India."

"We can't leave!" she cried. "If the reports are wrong, the family from Kharkhoda will come here to look for us!"

"They will be happy to find you gone," said Sardar firmly. "If they survived Kharkhoda, then they will manage to make it to Pakistan."

Cultural norms in this part of the world usually expect younger members of the family to step back and allow the elders to decide what should be done, but these elders had gone through so much it seemed to have paralysed their ability to act. Sardar took the reins into his own hands. In a while, his uncles and his aunt took their place by his side; together, they worked out a strategy and instructed everyone on what to do.

Sardar was adamant about taking along as many Muslims from nearby places as wished to go with them. The next day as dawn approached the two trucks, full of people, were ready to be on their way.

As they were leaving, Sardar took one last look around the room he was leaving. Everything was in its place, as it had been in his own home in Kharkhoda. He noticed that his aunt had thrown dust covers over the furniture as she probably was in the habit of doing before leaving the house for a few days. His lips curved in a bitter smile, coming back again did not seem likely. He wondered if his mother had done the same before leaving…

One has time to think when travelling long distances. Once again, Sardar told himself firmly that now was the time for rational action only. He must not allow grief to overpower him.

The return journey took ten days. Because there were so many of them, they were extra careful about not drawing attention to themselves: they took detours and longer routes where required, and when there were crowds present, some of them would lie down and allow themselves to be covered by a tarpaulin. A few times the drivers deposited half the passengers somewhere safe and doubled back to pick them up again when it was less crowded.

To return to Pakistan with still no surety about the fate of his immediate family was heartrending, but there is something about saving lives that brings inner peace. This was the third time Sardar had crossed the blood-drenched border between India and Pakistan, and only now did he possess the strength to live with uncertainty until further news.

14th October, 2016

Syed Sardar Ahmad:

"The morning I left Delhi for Aligarh was the same day my family in Kharkhoda left home. There were forty Hindu villages near our town and only one other Muslim settlement. As the political tension grew, these forty Hindu villages became hostile towards us. They collected volunteers, and they attacked my kasba. They did not prevail; we had ammunition to defend ourselves. My family planned to travel to Delhi from Kharkhoda; Delhi was 15 to 17 miles away. They were only four miles away from home when they were surrounded by thousands of men who were armed with all sorts of weapons. My family retreated back to the village for safety. Their attackers laid siege to the village for around ten days. The ammunition my people possessed was exhausted in those ten days. The other problem was that the access to water had been cut off; they could only rely on what they had inside, which was not enough. We were planning to leave so we were not stocking up on necessities like we ordinarily did.

The attack subsided; there was no incidence of shooting for a few days, so my family sent people to sneak around the outskirts to find out what was going on. They found out that the attackers had retreated to their homes. Assuming it was a good time to leave, they formed a large group. In the form of a *kafla*, the whole village set out. They could not run all the way to Delhi; they had to make stops. They stopped at a Hindu village, their only choice. Very early during their stay, they realised they would not be spared. As word spread about their stay, the attackers from other Hindu villages started to conjugate to attack again.

When they were attacked the biggest concern for the Muslims, for my family was the security of their women, the attackers might rape them. So my mother asked Mukhtar, my brother, who was younger than me, to kill her. He shot her. Mukhtar killed our mother with his own hands as per my mother's own request. My mother preferred she be killed by her own son than be misbehaved towards. This difficult choice was made by other women of my family and village, in fact it was made by women all across India. The rest kept fighting but were eventually overpowered and also killed.

Of this group of around three or four thousand or even more, only five men survived because they were buried under the dead bodies. The attackers thought they had killed everyone. The army came there after a day. They said that if anybody was alive, they should come out. Then, these people came out from under the dead bodies.

I think around five hundred of my family were martyred. See, in a family, there are a number of relations. It is like a tribe. They all died. My four brothers, my grandparents, and father, and my mother, these were the immediate members who were martyred there. The rest were close relatives. Everyone from Kharkhoda whom I had ever known growing up died in that massacre. My whole community was martyred.

Sabir Ali was one of the five survivors. He knew I too had survived; he had seen me. He got to know that we had settled in Jhang, he asked around about my whereabouts, and he arrived in Jhang around six months after we settled there. He is the one who narrated this story to me. I can imagine the horror they went through because I witnessed others going through that horror on my way to Pakistan. Throughout my journey, there were massacred bodies of Muslims; the massacres were instigated by Hindus, but they were executed by Sikhs. There were fields around the railway tracks which served as a perfect cover for Sikhs. Once we crossed Patiala there were four stations including Amritsar where the train stopped. We saw trains that had been stopped on the way; they were not being allowed access to food or water; neither were they being allowed safe passage. There were five trains from East Punjab that arrived with slaughtered Muslims; these are the ones I have first-hand knowledge of, I am sure there were more. This caused violence in West Punjab, where Muslims targeted Sikhs in retaliation. The Liaquat-Nehru Agreement was signed to settle this ensuing violence. **"**

To visualise these events is painful and to build around them with fiction would trivialise this monumentally tragic moment for many families. It has, therefore, not been attempted. It is retold as narrated by Sabir Ali, an eye witness to this mass killing.

Sardar's paternal grandfather, Meer Meherbaan Ali, was the first to be martyred when his family members were attacked.

When the family group was stopped, the attackers called for Meer Meherbaan Ali to step out, which he did. Meer Meherbaan Ali was a *numbardar*, a large landowner and the most powerful man in the neighbourhood. The attackers wished to make an example of him. They cut off his arms and then his legs in front of his family and all the other persons present. It is impossible to imagine the suffering of this man and of those who loved him and who witnessed this horrific event.

After that, they turned to the others.

18th October, 2016

Syed Sardar Ahmad:

"We reached Jallo to receive a warm welcome.
People were waiting with water and food for those
migrating from India. The enthusiasm and
generosity of spirit I saw that day I have not
witnessed again. It was when we reached Lahore
safe that the military on board told us that the
weapons they were carrying were not loaded.
They had not been given ammunition; if the train
had been attacked, they could not have defended
it. Most of the ammunition from Pakistan's
rightful share was destroyed.

I spent days searching for my family in camps and
on railway stations. Where we have Zaman Park
today, there are so many refugees buried.
Refugees coming on foot, donkey carts and bull
carts would reach mall road, have water and pass
away.

My aunt on my father's side, her husband and
their children, had moved to Jhang in December
1947, and they asked me to live with them. This
is why I settled in Jhang. This was around
December 1947. Z.A. Hashmi and his family
stayed on in Lahore.

I moved to Jhang from Lahore in December 1947,
after going back to Rohtak and bringing my
relatives from there.

For the next two years, I was not able to continue my education for economic reasons; in 1949, I was admitted to FC College in Lahore. I did my BA from there.

When the record of our lands in East Punjab was officially released in 1952, we were allotted land here in Pakistan; I remained busy looking after it. In 1954, I went to London and was admitted to Lincoln's Inn.

It had been my mother's earnest wish that I marry her sister's daughter. She wished for me to get a higher education. When I went to London to become a barrister-at-law, I became a son-in-law as well. I fulfilled both my mother's wishes. I got married in London in 1954.

I came back to Pakistan in 1957 and practised law in Jhang for ten years. In a murder case with the same situation, the same events, the same law, you can argue for this side or the other. My conscience did not allow me to continue in the profession. I had my lands, and I continued looking after them. I was pleased and satisfied with my life. I reaped what I sowed, and I have been content with that.**"**

Sardar turned to a small book in a brown leather binding that lay on a table by his chair, the single word: Ghalib etched onto it in gold. Sardar picked it up and turned the yellow pages. His grandfather loved Ghalib's poetry and had often read out his poems to his grandchildren.

He recalled, once, as they were getting ready to leave the house, already late for a wedding, Abba Jan had discovered *Dadajan* reading Ghalib's dewaan in his room.

"Abba Jan, der ho rahi hai aur aap Ghalib parh rahay hain," my father had chided his father.

"Mian, aam aur Ghalib ka koi khas waqt nahi hota," Meer Meherbaan Ali had replied. "You can eat mangoes and read Ghalib anytime."

"That was your grandfather's," Sardar turned to his daughter, Ameena, and spoke softly "He gave it to me to read, and I was never able to return it. It's yours now."

The memory had fatigued him. All these years had neither eased the pain of the loss nor the pain of being a helpless bystander to blood-shed.

18th October, 2016

Syed Sardar Ahmad:

> "At times, I can hear Apajan calling out to me in her soft voice; I hear Salar beckoning me; I hear Mukhtar bickering with me; I hear the playful laughter of Iftikhar and Waqar; I hear Abba Jan giving me his wise counsel; I hear my *Dadajan* reciting Ghalib to me. Standing on my zameen in Jhang, I feel a longing for Kharkhoda tug at my heart..."

Sab kahan, kuch, lala-o-gul mein numayan ho gayeen
Khak mein kya suratein hongi kay pinhan ho gayeen
Yaad thi hamko bhi ranga rang bazm aaraaiyan
Lekin ab naqsh o nigaar e taaq e nisiyaan ho gayeen

Now not all, but some may be seen as flowers and blooms
How many others are hidden in the dust, who knows?
I remember well those colourful gatherings
They are now but etchings in every corner of my mind

Mirza Ghalib

Part IV

OUTWARD TELEGRAM

From High Commissioner for
the United Kingdom

To COMMONWEALTH RELATIONS

    OFFICE

Repeated to

Sent 151750 MF

No. 762

Cypher

~~from~~

~~Clear~~

Signed by

Name in type A.C.B. SYMON

Time 15th September 1.30 p.m.

Priority IMMEDIATE   SECRET

MY TELEGRAM NO. 749 DATED 13TH SEPTEMBER.
COMMUNAL DISTURBANCES.

1. PUNJAB   FOLLOWING IS MAIN INFORMATION RECEIVED
DURING LAST TWO DAYS REGARDING SITUATION.

A) THERE WAS CONTINUED TENSION IN RURAL AREAS OF
EAST PUNJAB BUT MOVEMENT OF REFUGEES HAS CONTINUED
SATISFACTORILY.

B) IN AMBALA DISTRICT SITUATION WAS REPORTED TO
HAVE DETERIORATED GREATLY AND IN ROHTAK DISTRICT
HEAVY KILLING WAS REPORTED AT ONE PLACE (PLEASE
TREAT THIS PARA. AS CONFIDENTIAL).

A telegram announcing the heavy killing in Rohtak
District, presumably of Syed Sardar Ahmad's family and
others from his village

Kharkhoda, India, 1947

Meer Mehrbaan Ali, Grandfather of Syed Sardar Ahmad

Syed Sharif Ahmad, Father of Syed Sardar Ahmad

Syed Mukhtar Ahmad
Brother of Syed Sardar Ahmad

Syed Salar Ahmad
Brother of Syed Sardar Ahmad

Syed Iftikhar Ahmad
Brother of Syed Sardar Ahmad

Syed Waqar Ahmad
Brother of Syed Sardar Ahmad

Aligarh, 1936

ایک یادگار تصویر جو کھرکھودہ میں لی گئی

Left to right.
Sitting messrs:- Kanchi.
Jamal - Batakh - Matkila.
Standing messrs:- Kawwa - Galebi - thr mamelai -
Brus (bumba) Rangilla - Chatkila

Kharkhoda, India, 1947

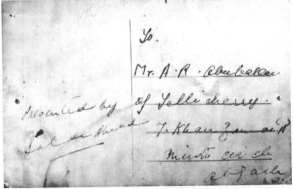

A postcard sent by Salar Ahmad to his teacher

Syed Sardar Ahmad with a young cousin

Kharkhoda, India, 1947

Syed Sardar Ahmad's Mamu Jan,
Professor Khawaja Manzoor Hossain with his family

Syed Sardar Ahmad's Khalu, Z. A. Hashmi with his family

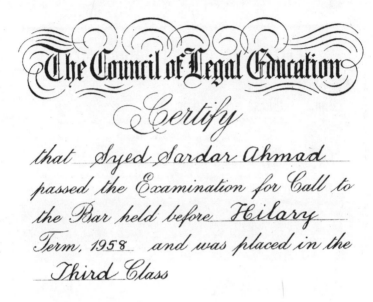

The Council of Legal Education

Certify

that *Syed Sardar Ahmad* passed the Examination for Call to the Bar held before *Hilary Term, 1958* and was placed in the *Third Class*

Dated the 17th day of *February 1958.*

Paul Tyne

Director.

Thomas Harwatt

Secretary.

February 1958, Lincoln's Inn Bar Exam

Certificate of Standing, &c.

Lincoln's Inn.

These are to Certify that *Syed Sardar Ahmad, B.A. of German Christian College, Lahore, and of 8 Cure Lines, Jhang Punjab, Pakistan, the first son of Syed Shariff Ahmad of 8 Cure Lines aforesaid, Landlord, deceased* was admitted into the Honourable Society of this Inn on the *sixteenth* day of *December* One thousand nine hundred and *fiftythree*, and was called to the Degree of an Utter Barrister, on the *fourth* day of *February* One thousand nine hundred and *fiftyeight*, hath paid all Dues and Duties to the Society, and that his deportment therein hath been proper.

In testimony whereof I have hereunto set my hand and the Seal of the said Society, this *fourth* day of *February*, in the year of our Lord One thousand nine hundred and *fiftyeight*.

Witness.   *Treasurer.*

H. C. H. Fairchild.

In the High Court of Justice.
Queen's Bench Division.

This is to Certify that *Syed Sardar Ahmad* of *Lincoln's Inn* has signed the Roll of Barristers of the High Court of Justice, Queen's Bench Division, for the present *Hilary* Sittings.

Dated the *5th* day of *February* 1958

A. Highmore King
Queen's Coroner and Attorney and Master of the Crown Office,
Royal Courts of Justice.

The above form of Certificate is for the use of Barristers who are going to any Colony by the Ordinances of which they may be required to produce a Certificate that they have signed the Roll of Barristers, but it is not necessary that Barristers intending to practise in England should sign the Roll of Barristers or obtain such Certificate.

If you, the within-named   , desire to sign the Roll of Barristers you must, at the time of applying to do so, produce the within-written Certificate that you have been called to the Bar; and if you desire to have a Certificate of having signed the Roll of Barristers, you must obtain the signature of the Queen's Coroner and Attorney and Master of the Crown Office to the above form of Certificate.

February 1958, Certificate of Standing, Lincoln's Inn

Mr & Mrs M. E. Rahman
request the pleasure of the company of

....

at the marriage of their daughter

Seemeen Mahtalaat

to

Syed Sardar Ahmad

at the

Islamic Cultural Centre,

Regent's Lodge, 146 Park Road, London, N.W.8

on Saturday, 21st August, 1954

at 5.30 p.m.

and afterwards at a Reception at the same place.

34 GRAND DRIVE,
RAYNES PARK,
    LONDON, S.W.20.   **R.S.V.P.**

Syed Sardar Ahmad's Wedding Invitation

Syed Sardar Ahmad with his newly-wed wife, Seemeen Mahtalat,
on their left is Mohammad Farid-ur-Rahman (Seemeen's younger brother)
on their right is Mohammad Noman-ur-Rahman (Seemeen's elder brother)

Sitting Mohammad Ehsan-ur-Rahman, Father of Seemeen
Sitting Midhat Bano, Mother of Seemeen, Sister of Riffat Bano

H. C. G. D. A. No. 6.   Printed by the Supdt. Govt. Ptg. West Pak., Lahore—1956.

XIII.A. *80 3*

In the High Court of West Pakistan, Lahore.

I, ___ABDUL KARIM_____ , Deputy Registrar of

the High Court of West Pakistan, Lahore, do hereby certify and

declare that ___Syed Sardar Ahmad_____

_____son of Syed Sharif Ahmad,_____

has this day been admitted and enrolled

as an Advocate of the High Court of West Pakistan, Lahore.

Given under my hand and the seal of the Court, this

___SIXTEENTH___ day of ___APRIL_____ in the year of

our Lord, one thousand nine hundred and ___FIFTYEIGHT.___

By order of the High Court.

Deputy Registrar

15/16-4-5-8

Note:— The condition of this certificate is that the holder shall
not take part in any seditious or disloyal movement.

April, 1958, Certificate of Advocate High Court of Lahore

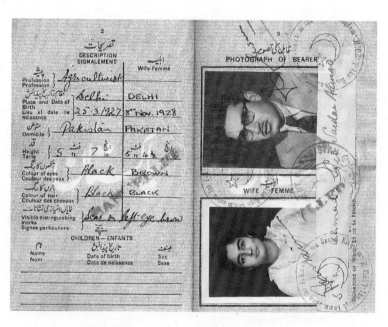

Passport of Syed Sardar Ahmad & Seemeen Mahtalat Ahmad

GOVERNMENT OF INDIA.

CERTIFICATE OF IDENTITY.

(1) Name: **Shreemati MM Midhat Bano Rahman**

(2) Father's/Husband's Name: M.E.Rahman

(3) Domicile: Indian

(4) Occupation: ---

(5) Age: 47 yrs.

(6) Place of birth: Kanend, Patiala State, PEPSU

(7) Permanent address: Ground fl., 'Hill Crest', 6 Carmichael, Road, Bombay 26.

e applicant:

mrs. midhat Bano Rahman

5 - 10 - 50

CERTIFIED THAT Shree/Shreemati **Midhat Bano** whose details are given above and **Rahman** whose photograph is duly affixed and certified by me, is a person domiciled in India, has continued to reside in this Country even after the partition and is not an evacuee. Certified further that the applicant is now going to Pakistan on a temporary visit for the purpose of **seeing brother & sister** and that there is no objection to his/her/their return to India.

This Certificate is valid for two months from the date of issue. The applicant is going along with/alone.

1. Daughter: Seemeen Mahtabart Rahman 22 yrs.

No. **2466** of 1950.

BOMBAY, dated:

GTB: 16/8

5th October 1950

GTB

And Collector of Bombay & Bombay Suburban District, Bombay.

Statement Allowing Midhat Bano and Seemeen Mahtalat, both Indian Citizens, to visit Pakistan. It also specifies that they should not be restricted to go back to India

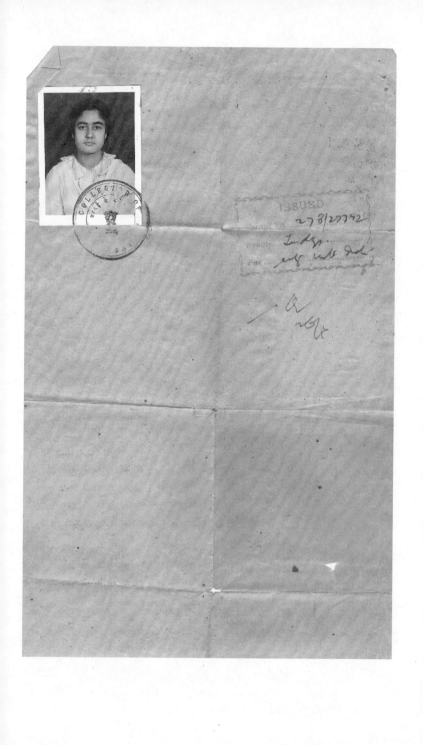

IN THE COURT OF T.M. RISCI ESQR. CLAIMS OFFICER
WARD NO. IV NAPIER BARRACKS KARACHI.

True Copy.

Karachi, 7-5-60.

1. Case No. Nil. 2. Registration No. 5818/IV

3. Applicant's name. 4. Father's name/Husband's name.
   Fatima Begum. S. Inayat Hussain.

5. Address in Pakistan. 6. Residence in Bharat,
   198, Lawrence Road, Pakistan Quarters Mohalla Barhaya, Kucha
   Karachi. Chelan, Delhi City.

7. Date of Arrival in Pakistan. 8. Reasons for migration.
   1-11-47. Civil Riots.

9. Location of property. 10. Details of evacuee property held
   Khura Rewari, Dist. Gurgaon. or occupied in Pakistan.
   -----Nil----

11. Value claimed. 12. Value verified.

    Schedule I - Rs. 3,000/- Schedule I - Rs. 1,728/-
    Schedule VI-Rs. 3,537/- Schedule VI-Rs. 480/-
    Schedule V - Rs. 9,600/- Schedule V. 47 . 40 acres.

VERIFICATION ORDER.

This claim case No. 5818/IV valued Rs. 3,000/- is preferred by
Mst. Fatima Begum under Schedule I in respect of her share ina a
residential house situated in Rewari and also her share in agricultural
property described under Shedule V under Schedule VI she has claimed
Rs.5/- p.m. as her share in the house. Her son Hamid Hussain appeared
as attorney and examined. Power of attorney stands on Part 'A' of
the file. It is said the claimant migrated to Pakistan with her son
who is attorney in this case in 1947 from Delhi at the time of Pati-
tion. Ext. 1 is certificate of attorney's department and Ext. 2 is
an affidavit. On the basis of these documents I declare the claimant
displaced person.

Schedule I. :- The claimant are five sisters of whome Farhatunnisa
claim case No. 975/V and Case No. 4030/II have already been verified
In Claim Case No. 4030/II the learned Claims Officer has verified
the value of the house for Rs. 8640/- at the rate of Rs. 18/- p.m. the
claimant's 1/5th share comes to Rs. 1,728/- according to this
assessment which is allowed.

Schedule VI.:- According to verification order in claim case No.
4030/II Schedule VI is allowed for 10 years which comes to Rs. 480/-
only to the extent of 1/5th Share. This is exhibited No. 3 in this
file.

P.T.O.

Schedule V. :- As per Ext. 4 the learned Claims Officer Mr. Azizi uddin has verified Farhatunnisa, Claimant's share in several villages of Milahabad District Lucknow to the extent of 47.40 acres which I also allow in the present case.

The claims thus verified under Schedule I for ℞ 1,728/- and under Schedule VI for ℞ 480/- and also under Schedule V for 47.40 acres of proprietory rights in tenant cultivated cannal irrigaged agricultural land situated in various villages of Malehabad district Lucknow U.P. India within the rainfal range of 31" to 40" per annum.

sd/-
(T. M. Risci)
Claims Officer Ward IV.

```
{----------------------------------------{
{                                        {
{         CLAIMS OFFICER, KARACHI.       {
{ Date of Order...........7-5-60.        {
{ Application made on......10-5-60.      {
{ Stamps called for ℞.....2/-/-          {
{ stamps supplied on......27-5-60.       {
{ Copy ready on-----------27-5-60.       {
{ Copy delivered on.......27-5-60.       {
{                                        {
{                    sd/-                {
{              Senior Clerk.             {
{  sd/-                                  {
{ Copiest.                               {
{----------------------------------------{
```

Damage Caused by Floods.

About 15000 people took shelter at station & other places near mandi & our kothi. It is a view of station.

Dead body guarded by a mughiana police man.

چاہ رہے سودالہ کینئے؟

وہ شتیک جگہ پیلا خان نے آور ذکروا پر از زے سے۔
یہ دائر شتیک ٹونگاگل سوبہ سامہ میں ٹو نہ از نساک
علینہا پرواقہ سے۔ ٹونگاگل کوہ سراس فشیرہ
میں کگ عاصلہ پرسے۔ اور بہاں سے کوہ سرگ کگ چا بان
مستا کیا جا تا سے۔

24.8.52

People are leaving
their homes in maghiana
due to flood.

A horse sinking because
poor animal can't resist in
such a fast flow of water.

Flood water near
mandi & Dur Kothi.

Flood ruins the main
bazar of Maghiana.

wheat was provided
to the flood
Deputy Commissioner distributes

شاداب کی مسجد اور سیکریٹیریٹ نزیل کے اردگرد
شاداب کو آئی گذشتہ میں گھِر گئی

Morning of 2nd Sept. 1950

Majumua

S. Sardar Ah——
M. U. Aligarh (U.P.)
India
1.3.1948.

مسجدِ شہدا

سرِ خاکِ شہید سے برگ ہائے لالہ می یا شم

کہ خونش با نہالِ ملّتِ ما ساز گار آمد

اُن ہزاروں شہیدوں کے نام جنہیں قیامِ پاکستان کے وقت بھارت کے
سکھ اور ہندو کفار نے محض مُسلمان ہونے اور حصولِ پاکستان کی جدّ و جہد میں
پیش پیش ہونے کی پاداش میں بربریت کا نشانہ بنایا اور شہید کیا ۔

اِن شہدائے تحریکِ پاکستان میں سیّد والد امیر سیّد مہربان علی میر سیّد رشید احمد
میرا والد میر شیّد شریف احمد میری والدہ ماجدہ میر چاروں بھائی
سیّد مختار احمد ۔ سیّد سالار احمد سیّد افتخار احمد اور سیّد وقار احمد
و دیگر عزیز و اقارب بھی شامل ہیں ۔

خدا رحمت کُند ایں عاشقان پاک طینت را

مورخہ ۹ ستمبر ۱۹۹۶ء   تعمیر بجانب : بریگیڈیئر سیّد سردار احمد

Khutba Masjid-e-Shuhada

Part V

A Daughter's Note...

As my father said, when his generation handed over Pakistan to its children, it was a reanimated country, full of potential. We, its new custodians, never experienced the agonies of this country's conception, and we, therefore, cannot imagine the anguish the Muslims of my father's generation went through during the Partition of India. In 1947, they took this land as a parent would an injured child from the brink of death. We barely know the sufferings of those people who gave their blood, so this country would live before it was handed over to us.

We cannot know, my father said, how much those Muslims sacrificed for their new homeland, how much they left behind — their loved ones, their settled lives, and comforts, for this new entity. They had all rejected an uncertain future in undivided India, one in which they saw their children being marginalised.

They had no idea how their new home would treat them or how they would survive here. Despite their sacrifices, their new homeland would turn out as they hoped it would, or they would be disappointed? They felt that here they might have a chance, and here their children would be safe. All they had to hold on to this path was this hope and their unwavering trust in Allah. The willingness to act by means of His support to take this chance to chase a dream until it was achieved.

My father would often refer to a Tibetan saying in, "Tragedy should be utilised as a source of strength, no matter what sort of difficulties, how painful experience is, if we lose our hope, that's our real disaster."

Hence, this book, which tells the story of my father. It documents his sacrifices and those that others of his generation made for Pakistan. These sacrifices may be known and remembered by generations to come.

Every day of his life, I saw my father mourn those he lost. I saw him be grateful for what he was blessed with, but his gratitude did not lessen the pain of the nineteen day's journey he made to Pakistan. They say tragedy can last a lifetime, and I saw my father wilfully fight the sense of loss this tragedy had given him. In his last few days, he was grasping for the last few breaths, and I could hear him call out to Salar, his brother whose legacy I hope lives on in his grandson, my son, Salar.

It is almost impossible to imagine because it is so painful, the life of a young man of twenty-one who finds himself the sole surviving member of a large, close-knit family; a young man alone in a new country. At such a formative age, he needed to make a life for himself with all the decisions that go with it. It took immense courage, but my father was a fighter. With the help of the Lord in Whom he never failed to trust, he did not let his personal losses force him into giving up. He carved out a future for himself and his new family; he managed to give us the love and security we could so easily have never known. For this, as for so many other things, we bless him and remember him.

It is as Maya Angelou said, "At the end of the day people won't remember what you said or did, they will remember how you made them feel."

Life means heading inexorably towards death while we still breathe, progressing towards the end of the time allotted to us by our Ultimate Master. When that time runs out, we move onto the next stage. It happens to all living things; they live, and they die, and then they are gone. Some people, however, are special, they fight their battles, they conquer every hurdle to become larger than life each time, and so they live on past their time on this earth.

Their journey is extraordinary; they remain in peoples' hearts and memories forever...that was my father, Syed Sardar Ahmad. May his sacrifices bear fruit, Amen.

Ameena Ahmad

Syed Sardar with his daughter Ameena Ahmad

Syed Sardar Ahmad with his daughter, Ameena, wife, Seemeen,
son-in-law, Kashif, and granddaughter, Eeshal.

Syed Sardar with his grandchildren, who he hoped would continue
his legacy of patriotism

Syed Sardar with the family that survives him

Syed Sardar Ahmad with his wife, Seemeen Mahtalat Ahmad

In September 2016, Syed Sardar Ahmad was interviewed at his residence in Lahore; the interview was conducted and transcribed courtesy of the Citizen's Archive of Pakistan.

The year following this interview, on the 13th of October 2017, Syed Sardar Ahmad passed away. The following year, on the 12th of August, his wife Seemeen Mahtalat Ahmad breathed her last.

They are survived by a daughter, Ameena Ahmad, who is married to Syed Kashif H. Gardezi and they have three beautiful children, Eeshal, Salar, and Suleman.